CANAAN DOG

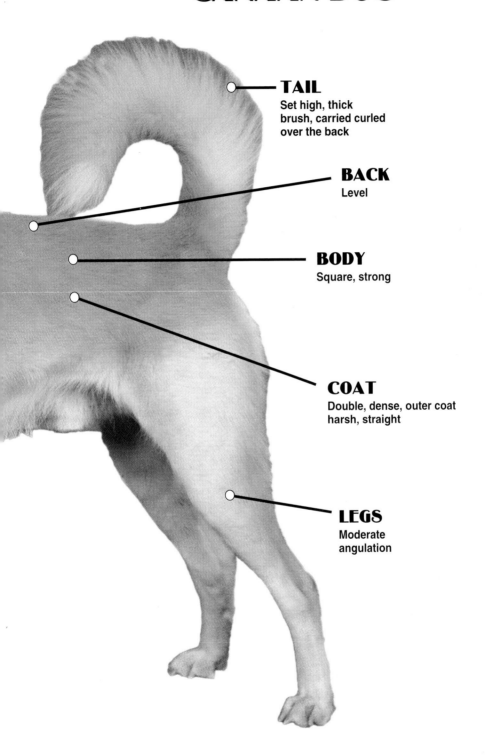

TAIL
Set high, thick
brush, carried curled
over the back

BACK
Level

BODY
Square, strong

COAT
Double, dense, outer coat
harsh, straight

LEGS
Moderate
angulation

Title page: U-AGII Keely's Girl Tobie, NA, CGC, photographed by Lee Boyd.

Photographers: Sari Alanko, Terry Bagley, Kathy and Michael Bogner, Katryna Bogovich, Lee Boyd, Caren and Russ Curtiss, Donna Drabik, Isabelle Francais, Christine and David Franklin, Sheryl Glass, Arthur and Marian Goldberg, Avi Goldberg, Jerry and Cheryl Hennings, Victor Kaftal, Yigal Pardo, Dana Pittman, Sara Nugent, Myrna Shiboleth, Jill and Ian Terry, Walden Photo, Isabella Zirri

© T.F.H. Publications, Inc.

Distributed in the UNITED STATES to the Pet Trade by T.F.H. Publications, Inc., 1 TFH Plaza, Neptune City, NJ 07753; on the Internet at www.tfh.com; in CANADA by Rolf C. Hagen Inc., 3225 Sartelon St., Montreal, Quebec H4R 1E8; Pet Trade by H & L Pet Supplies Inc., 27 Kingston Crescent, Kitchener, Ontario N2B 2T6; in ENGLAND by T.F.H. Publications, PO Box 74, Havant PO9 5TT; in AUSTRALIA AND THE SOUTH PACIFIC by T.F.H. (Australia), Pty. Ltd., Box 149, Brookvale 2100 N.S.W., Australia; in NEW ZEALAND by Brooklands Aquarium Ltd., 5 McGiven Drive, New Plymouth, RD1 New Zealand; in SOUTH AFRICA by Rolf C. Hagen S.A. (PTY.) LTD., P.O. Box 201199, Durban North 4016, South Africa; in JAPAN by T.F.H. Publications. Published by T.F.H. Publications, Inc.

MANUFACTURED IN THE
UNITED STATES OF AMERICA
BY T.F.H. PUBLICATIONS, INC.

CANAAN DOG

A COMPLETE AND RELIABLE HANDBOOK

Lee Boyd and Victor Kaftal

RX-150

CONTENTS

ORIGIN AND HISTORY OF THE CANAAN DOG

ORIGIN

The Canaan Dog belongs to the class of primitive breeds called *pariah dogs*, which includes dogs such as the Basenji, Dingo, Ibizan Hound, New Guinea Singing Dog, and Pharaoh Hound, among others. Pariah dogs live partly in free-roaming packs in the wilderness, partly at the fringe of civilization where they scavenge from human settlements, and partly in domestication. They are found across large stretches of Asia, from the Middle East to the Indian subcontinent and to South East Asia, and also in North and Central Africa, Australia, and the Americas.

The Canaan Dog belongs to the class of primitive breeds called "pariah dogs," which live partly in free-roaming packs in the wilderness and partly in domestication.

Very little is known about the origin of pariah dogs. They are considered very ancient and close to the original ancestor of the dog species, the wolf. Some authorities hypothesize that most dog breeds have evolved from pariah dogs, but only DNA testing will eventually be able to sort out the relationships between the various pariah dogs and the modern dog breeds.

Morphologically, most pariah dogs belong to the Spitz family. They are medium-sized dogs, fairly square in proportion, with a double coat, a tail curled over the back, a wedge-shaped head, prick ears, and a characteristic short, quick trot.

Canaan Dogs are a specific variety of pariah dog found in the Middle East, and more specifically in Israel and surrounding regions, including Jordan, Lebanon, and the Sinai peninsula. Canaan Dogs, or dogs very similar to them, have also been found in parts of Egypt and North Africa, as well as in Syria and Iraq.

The Canaan Dog falls somewhere in the middle of the range of pariah-dog types—they are not as large, heavy boned, and heavy coated as the shepherd-type pariah dogs living in the mountain areas to the north of Israel, but also not as light boned and refined as the sighthound types south of Israel.

While Canaan Dogs have much more variability than many of the "human-made" dog breeds, they have a fairly distinctive type, and even today, free-roaming packs of relatively similar appearance can be found in the deserts of Israel.

Canaan Dogs are still common around Bedouin settlements. Bedouins often capture male pups from nearby dens and leave females to fend for themselves, loosely following the camp and its dogs. Since time immemorial, Bedouins have used Canaans to guard their flocks and camps, thus harnessing the strong territorial instincts of these dogs.

Canaan Dogs also lived for centuries in Arab villages, mainly used as guard dogs, but even there they were never much removed from nature.

To understand Canaan Dogs, then, it is essential to keep in mind that, contrary to the great majority of dog breeds that have been selectively bred by humans to serve some working or companionship purpose, Canaans have been molded almost exclusively by natural selection to survive in their harsh environment.

They are indeed ideally suited to their original geographical area, which encompasses rocky deserts, hilly wilderness, and low mountains, and a wide range of temperatures and climates— from the fierce heat of the day in the desert to the night freezes in the mountains. Most of their physical and temperamental characteristics and their keen senses can be interpreted as direct adaptations to their surroundings.

HISTORY

The Bible mentions a local dog called *Kelev Kana'ni*— that's where the breed got its name. Prebiblical drawings and carvings depicting dogs that are indistinguishable from modern-day Canaans have been found in the Beni Hassan tombs of about 2000 BC and in many other rock carvings in the area. Skeletons from the first millennium BC found in the large dog burials at Ashkelon in southern Israel also fit the modern breed's characteristics.

According to tradition, at the time of the Diaspora when the Israelites were forcefully removed from their country, they had to leave behind their dogs. These dogs reverted to the wild and formed the packs of pariah dogs that most likely roamed the area then just as they do now. Much more recently, Golan Heights villagers escaped to Syria during the Six Day War in 1967, and their abandoned dogs assembled in packs and reverted to the wild.

Until the large-scale Jewish immigration to Palestine began at the start of this century, the region was very scarcely populated and the majority of Canaan Dogs lived in wild packs. Since then, their number has been

Dr. Rudolphina Menzel, a cynologist interested in studying and preserving pariah dogs, is responsible for the rise of the Canaan Dog as a modern breed. Isr. Ch. Laish me Bnei HaBitachon, bred by Dr. Menzel, is the first Israeli champion Canaan and still one of the best specimens of the breed.

greatly reduced by the encroachment of civilization, and free-living packs are now increasingly rare. Also, Arab villagers and some Bedouins have started importing other dog breeds. Mongrelization and rabies control have further reduced the number of "pure" Canaan Dogs.

Fortunately for the Canaan Dog, a Viennese cynologist, Professor Rudolphina Menzel, immigrated to Palestine in 1934. She was interested in studying and preserving the local pariah dogs. The Haganah, Israel's first defense force, needed a service dog able to withstand the harsh Middle Eastern climate. This conjoining of interests gave rise to the Canaan Dog as a modern breed—the only breed originating in Israel.

Dr. Menzel started capturing litters of puppies and adult Canaans. It is fascinating to read her account of how she attracted the first adult, Dugma, into her yard using a bitch in heat as a lure. A few weeks later, she was already able to take him on the bus and walk him on the busy streets of Haifa.

She acquired other Canaan Dogs from Arab or Druse villagers, and thus a small-scale breeding program was started. In this way, she founded the modern breed. The Canaan Dog was used extensively during and after Israel's War of Independence for patrol, tracking, and guard duties. Hagar, a wild-born Canaan bitch, was the first dog on record to be trained to detect land mines. After 1948, Professor Menzel housed her breeding program in a seeing-eye dog institute and successfully managed to train some Canaans for that task—a remarkable feat, given the natural suspiciousness of the breed.

Meanwhile, the breed acquired recognition from the Israeli dog fancy. The first Canaan Dog standard, created by Dr. Menzel, was accepted by the Israel Kennel Club in 1953. Soon after, the Canaan Dog was adopted as the national breed of Israel. The breed was then recognized by the Federation Cynologique Internationale (FCI) in 1966 and was placed in the Spitz and Primitive Breeds group. The breed was also introduced into several European countries, South Africa, the US, and Canada.

Currently, the population of Canaan Dogs in North America equals that of the domesticated population in Israel. Besides Israel and North America, other major breeding centers of Canaan Dogs are in England, Finland, and Italy. Canaans are also found in Bermuda, Germany, Switzerland, and a few other countries. Not counting Bedouin and free-living packs, we estimate that there are about 1,000 living Canaan Dogs in the world. This is definitely a rare breed and care must be taken to properly manage its relatively small gene pool.

Israel is still the center of the Canaan Dog community, with a large number of domesticated dogs, experienced judges, international Canaan Dog shows/symposia, and a small but genetically important population of free-living and Bedouin dogs that are added in a controlled way to the breeding program. Many domesticated Canaan Dogs today have at least one free-living ancestor within five to seven generations.

CANAAN DOGS IN NORTH AMERICA

The first four Canaan Dogs were imported into the US by Ursula Berkowitz of Oxnard, California, in 1965. They were Toro me Isfajah, bred by a Druse tribe; Waf me Massada, acquired from a Bedouin tribe; and Birion me Bnei HaBitachon and Belith of Bnei HaBitachon, bred by Dr. Menzel. After these, many more imports followed, local breeding programs started, and the population of Canaan Dogs in the US and Canada grew over the years.

Although Canaan Dogs are still far from a popular breed, their increasing numbers brought them recognition by the main dog registries of North America. The United Kennel Club recognized Canaan Dogs in 1992 and has placed them in the Sighthounds and Pariah Dogs Group. The Canadian Kennel Club took them into their Working Group in 1993. The breed entered the American Kennel Club's Herding Group in 1997. In the UK, The Kennel Club has placed the breed in the Utility Group. Many Canaans are now shown in conformation shows, and obedience, agility, tracking, and herding trials.

As is usual with most breeds imported into the US, type differences with the country of origin and within the US have evolved, but continuing importation of Canaan Dogs has helped to maintain a strong representation of the Israeli type.

Both the authors of this book belong to the Israel Canaan Dog Club of America (ICDCA)—one of only four Canaan Dog clubs in the world. If you are interested in finding out more about the ICDCA, becoming a member, or receiving breeder referrals, you can write to ICDCA, 2739 Navaho Ave., Denver, IA 50622, or visit the ICDCA web site (www.itb.it/canaan/icdca). In the UK, you can contact the Canaan Dog Club, 113 Cranleigh Road, Feltham, Middlesex, England TW13 4QA, Tel. 0181 384 5896.

DESCRIPTION OF THE CANAAN DOG

The Canaan Dog has not been selectively bred by humans to fulfill some purpose—it has evolved to survive in a harsh wilderness environment. Their medium size and athletic build gives Canaan Dogs the agility and stamina necessary to hunt the small- to medium-sized prey that they feed on and to stand down their natural competitors, such as wolves, hyenas, leopards, and jackals (all but the latter are almost completely extinct in Israel). At the same time, medium-sized dogs need less food and water than larger ones and dissipate body heat more easily.

In the desert, the sun is very strong and the glare is blinding. As a consequence, Canaans have developed dark eye pigmentation, dark eye rims, and dark noses. Some Canaans have a pink nose that darkens if exposed to enough sun—a snow nose—and this is a minor fault.

As with other wild dogs, Canaan Dogs have prick ears for the best collection of sound and for the greatest range of motion for postural communications. It is amazing how expressive Canaans can be with their ears! Occasionally, one or both ears will fail to stand completely, and after the dog is one year old, this is considered a major conformational fault in the show ring.

Energy efficiency, difficult terrain, and a need to cover long distances in search of food and water require good movement; therefore, Canaans have evolved a square body with moderate angulation of the limbs, which permits them to trot effortlessly for hours. Their deep, moderately broad chest creates enough room for heart and lungs sufficient to sustain such levels of activity.

Their cat-like feet carry them efficiently through the rocky terrain of their environment, and their strong nails are perfect for digging dens and rooting rodents out of burrows (as well as for digging holes in manicured lawns, as so many Canaan owners have discovered to their dismay).

Their high-set bushy tail unfurls to act as a counterbalance during high-speed chases, and during cold nights, it covers their nose to filter the frigid air. Their harsh outer coat of guard hair protects them from the elements—winter is very cold and rainy in the hills of northern Israel. The soft, downy undercoat provides insulation from the cold as well as from the heat of the day and makes them extremely adaptable to all kinds of climates. We have seen Canaan puppies just flown in from Israel happily playing in the snow in subzero temperatures.

Their colors are also an adaptation to their environment. The black and white coloration is more common in northern Israel, where it disappears among the shadows cast by the limestones and basalts of the hills. The tawny colors blend easily among the sandstones of southern Israel.

The Canaan Dog is a medium-sized, square dog, with a thick tail curled over his back, a wedge-shaped head, prick ears, and a characteristic short, quick trot. Amos of Four Gables, owned by Daniel Archer.

DESCRIPTION

The Canaan Dogs' temperament is better understood by considering their life in the wild. Canaans have to compete with other predators, not to mention other feral or half-feral dog packs. As a consequence, domestic Canaans exhibit strong territoriality, a very developed guarding instinct, and a tendency to dog aggressiveness.

The need to fend for themselves explains their independence and self-reliance. Pack and social instincts extend to their human pack—your household—and make them affectionate and attached to their owners.

Natural selection favors strong-willed, dominant dogs. In the pack, often only the alpha pair breeds, so we see more dominance problems with Canaans than with many dogs bred for working or companionship purposes.

Living at the fringe of civilization, scavenging from humans that might tolerate or encourage them but might also unexpectedly turn against them, and being constantly exposed to a dangerous environment, Canaans have developed a very strong survival instinct. This shows itself often as a wariness of strangers and unusual objects or situations. Some Canaans with overdeveloped survival instincts are outright skittish.

Not addressed by the standards, but equally important, are the physiological adaptations of the breed. The Canaan Dogs' metabolism is remarkable. They are exceptionally efficient in using water: A study measured a daily water secretion of 1.8 percent of body weight as compared to a 3.5 percent usage for Pointers. Canaans are very efficient in dissipating body heat: 63 percent versus only 45 percent for Pointers. They are also more tolerant of brackish (salty) waters than other breeds, and like other wild animals, they can survive with little food for longer times.

They have lower metabolic rates than other breeds, and they share the amazing capability of many wild animals to pass with ease from extended periods of inactivity to sustained prolonged efforts. At home, this means that they are equally happy to be a lazy couch potato for most of the week and to turn into an indefatigable jogging companion on the weekend.

The natural selection to which Canaans have been subjected for so many centuries has turned them into a remarkably healthy and long-lived breed. A 14- to 15-year life span is normal. Several Canaans are known to have passed 17 years of age, and even more remarkable, a healthy 12-year-old Canaan is often active, fully alert, and not at all ready to retire.

STANDARD FOR THE CANAAN DOG

The Federation Cynologique Internationale (FCI) has accepted the Canaan Dog standard as set by the country of origin, Israel.

THE FCI STANDARD FOR THE CANAAN DOG
Revised November 28, 1985
Standard of the Israel Canaan Dog, Israeli Breed

General Appearance

A medium-sized, well balanced, strong and square dog resembling the wild dog type. Strong distinction between the sexes.

The Canaan Dog has a square body, with a level back, deep chest, well-tucked-up belly, and moderate angulation. U-UD Ch. Lahatut me Shaar Hagai, UD, CKC-CDX, TT, "Gil," owned by Victor Kaftal.

Head

Well proportioned, blunt wedge shape of medium length, appearing broader due to low set ears. Skull somewhat flattened. Some width allowed in powerful male heads. Stop shallow but defined. Muzzle sturdy, of moderate length and breadth. Jaws should be strong. Lips tight. Nose black.

Ears

Erect, relatively short and broad, slightly rounded at the tip and set low.

Eyes

Dark brown, slightly slanted, almond shaped. Dark rims essential.

Mouth

Full dentition with scissors or level bite.

Neck

Muscular, of medium length.

Body

Square, withers well developed, back level, loins muscular, chest deep and of moderate breadth, ribs well sprung. Belly well tucked up. Moderate angulation. Balance is essential.

Forequarters

The shoulder should be oblique and muscular, elbows close to the body. Forelegs perfectly straight.

Hindquarters

Powerful, well bent stifles. Hocks well let down. Strong buttocks, lightly feathered.

Feet

Strong, round and catlike with hard pads.

Tail

Set high, thick brush carried curled over the back.

Coat

Outer coat dense, harsh and straight, of short to medium length. Undercoat close and profuse.

Colour

Sand to red-brown, white, black, or spotted, with or without mask. If masked, mask must be symmetrical. Black mask permitted on all colours. White markings are permitted on all colours: "Boston Terrier" patterns are common. Grey, brindle, black-and-tan, or tricolour are unacceptable. Desert colours—sand, gold, red, cream—are most typical of the breed.

Weight and size

Height 50-60 cm, (20-24 in.), males may be considerably larger than females. Weight 18-25 kg. (40-55 lb.)

Gait

Quick, light and energetic trot. Should demonstrate marked agility and stamina. Correct movement is essential.

Character

Alert, quick to react, distrustful of strangers, strongly defensive but not naturally aggressive. Vigilant not only against man but other animals as well. Extraordinarily devoted and amenable to training.

Faults

All deviations from the standard of the breed. All faults in body structure which constitute a deviation from the norm of a well built dog; anything that would detract from his potential for survival as a desert animal.

N.B.: Male animals should have two apparently normal testicles fully descended into the scrotum.

Most other world Canaan Dog standards are based on the FCI standard. In particular, the United Kennel Club (UKC) standard is a faithful rendition of the FCI standard. The one major exception is the American Kennel Club (AKC) standard.

The main differences between the FCI and AKC standards are that the AKC standard calls for longer dogs, prescribes lower tail sets, and accepts smaller sized dogs. It calls for dogs with a flatter coat, which results from less undercoat. It explicitly accepts liver-colored dogs and tacitly accepts the black and tan color

AKC/UKC Ch. Bay Path's Amitz, CGC, owned by Jerry and Cheryl Hennings and Sandra Fournier.

pattern, which are both unacceptable under the FCI standard. On the other hand, the AKC standard disqualifies the all-white dog, which is a perfectly acceptable color to the FCI.

THE AKC STANDARD FOR THE CANAAN DOG

(Revised in 1996, prior to acceptance into the Herding Group.)

General Appearance—The Canaan Dog is a herding and flock guardian dog native to the Middle East. He is aloof with strangers, inquisitive, loyal and loving with his family. His medium-size, square body is without extremes, showing a clear, sharp outline. The Canaan Dog moves with athletic agility and grace in a quick, brisk, ground-covering trot. He has a wedge-shaped head with low-set erect ears, a bushy tail that curls over the back when excited, and a straight, harsh, flat-lying double coat.

Size, Proportion, Substance—*Size*—Height at the withers is 20 to 24 inches for dogs and 19 to 23 inches for bitches. The ideal Canaan Dog lies in the middle of the stated ranges. *Disqualifications—Dogs less than 20 inches or more than 25 inches. Bitches less than 18 inches or more than 23 inches. Proportion*—Square when measured from the point of the withers to the base of the tail and from the point of the withers to the ground. *Substance*—Moderate. Dogs generally weigh 45 to 55 pounds and bitches approximately 35 to 45 pounds. Dogs distinctly masculine without coarseness and bitches feminine without over-refinement.

Head—Elongated, the length exceeding the breadth and depth considerably. Wedge-shaped, when viewed from above. Slightly arched when viewed from the side, tapering to stop. The region of the forehead is of medium width, but appearing broader through ears set low to complete an alert expression, with a slight furrow between the eyes. *Expression*—Alert, watchful and inquisitive. Dignified. *Eyes*—Dark, almond-shaped, slightly slanted. Varying shades of hazel with liver-pointed dogs. Eye rims darkly pigmented or of varying shades of liver harmonizing with coat color. Fault—Unpigmented eye rims. *Ears*—Erect, medium to large, set moderately low, broad at the base, tapering to a very slightly rounded tip. Ears angled very slightly forward when excited. A straight line from the inner corner of the ear to the tip of the nose should just touch the inner corner of the eye and a line drawn from the tip of the ear to the tip of the nose should just touch the outer corner of the eye. Ear motion contributes to expression and clearly defines the mood of the dog. Major Fault—In the adult dog, other than erect ears. *Stop*—Slightly accentuated. *Muzzle*— Tapering to complete the wedge shape of the head. Length equal to or slightly longer than the length of the skull from the occiput to stop. Whisker trimming optional. *Nose*—Darkly pigmented or varying shades of liver, harmonizing with coat color. *Lips*—Tight with good pigmentation. *Bite*—Scissors.

Neck, Topline, Body—*Neck*—well arched. Balance to body and head and free from throatiness. *Topline*— Level with slight arch over the loins. *Body*—Strong, displaying athletic agility and trimness. *Chest*—Moderately broad and deep, extending to the elbows, with well-sprung ribs. *Loin*—Well-tucked-up. Short, muscled flanks. *Tail*—Set moderately high. May be carried curled over the back when excited; limited to one full curl. When extended, the bone must reach to the hocks. Fault—Tail which falls over to either side of the back.

Forequarters—Shoulders moderately angulated. Legs straight. Pasterns flexible with very slight slope when viewed from the side. Dewclaws may be removed. *Feet*—Catlike, pads hard, pigmentation harmonizing with nose and eye rims. Nails strong, hard, pigmentation harmonizing with either nose and eye rims or coat.

Hindquarters—Moderately angulated. In balance with forequarters. Straight when viewed from the rear. Thigh musculature well-developed, moderately broad. Hocks well let-down. Dewclaws must be removed. Feet and nails as in forequarters.

Coat—Double coat. Outer coat—straight, harsh, flat-lying, with slight ruff. Ruff more pronounced on males. Length of outer coat 1/2 to 1 1/2 inch; longer on ruff and back of thighs, shorter on body, legs and head. Under-

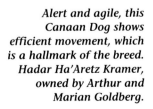

Alert and agile, this Canaan Dog shows efficient movement, which is a hallmark of the breed. Hadar Ha'Aretz Kramer, owned by Arthur and Marian Goldberg.

coat—straight, soft, short, flat-lying, density varying with climate. Tail bushy, increasing in plumage from set to end of bones, then tapering to pointed tip. Faults—Excessively long guard coat that masks the clean outline of the dog. Any trimming that alters the natural appearance of the dog.

Color—There are two color patterns. Pattern 1) Predominantly white with mask and with or without additional patches of color (large body patches are desirable). Pattern 2) Solid colored with or without white trim. Color may range from black through all shades of brown—sandy to red or liver. Shadings of black on a solid brown or tan dog are frequently seen. The trim on a solid colored dog may include chest, undercarriage, feet and lower part of leg and tip of tail. In all color patterns self-ticking may be present. *Disqualifications—a) Gray and/or brindle. b) All white.*

Mask—The mask is a desired and distinguishing feature of the predominantly white Canaan Dog. The mask is the same color(s) as the body patches on the dog. The basically symmetrical mask must completely cover the eyes and ears or can completely cover the head as in a hood. The only allowed white in the mask or hood is a white blaze of any size or shape and/or white on the muzzle below the mask. Faults—On predominantly white dogs—absence of mask, half mask, or grossly asymmetrical mask.

Gait—Movement is very important. Good reach and drive. Quick, brisk natural trot, apparently tireless, indicating an animal capable of trotting for hours. Covers ground more quickly than expected. Agile, able to change directions almost instantaneously. Tends to single-track at high speed. Fault—Anything that detracts from efficient movement.

Temperament—Alert, vigilant, devoted and docile with his family. Reserved and aloof with strangers. Highly territorial, serving as a responsive companion and natural guardian. Very vocal, persistent. Easily trained. Faults—Shyness or dominance toward people.

DISQUALIFICATIONS

Dogs less than 20 inches or more than 25 inches.
Bitches less than 18 inches or more than 23 inches.
Gray and/or brindle.
All white.
Approved: June 10, 1996
Effective: August 12, 1997

BREED REQUIREMENTS

EXERCISE

There are some breeds that need a large amount of daily exercise to avoid boredom, and other breeds that are physically incapable of strenuous exercise. One of the wonderful characteristics of Canaan Dogs is that they fall in the middle of this spectrum, because nature puts a premium on economy. Therefore, Canaan Dogs have a lot of stamina and enjoy exercise but are also content to be couch potatoes at other times. They make ideal running companions and are also well-suited to those who like to hike.

Give your Canaan an opportunity for daily exercise in order to keep him physically and mentally fit. These puppies receive both a workout and mental stimulation through play.

If such activities are not part of your normal lifestyle, you will want to find ways in which to give your Canaan Dog some opportunity for daily exercise in order to keep him fit. Also, this is an intelligent breed and mental stimulation is essential. Walking with your dog or participating in more structured endeavors such as obedience, tracking, or

agility will enrich your relationship with your dog, as well as meeting his physical and mental needs.

Puppies, too, need exercise and mental stimulation. Some common sense is in order. As is true for any breed, puppies should not be asked to jump very high before they have matured physically, their bones have hardened, their joints have tightened, and their coordination has developed, so that they are able to stand up to the stress of jumping. Puppies jump while playing, which is not a cause for concern. Rather, it is jumping unnaturally on hard surfaces and repetition that is the problem.

GROOMING

The Canaan Dog is the original wash-and-wear dog. Rarely do you see a brush at ringside! The dogs are shown in a natural condition. They don't require the hours of primping spent on some other breeds in order to be shown. Throughout most of the year, all they need is weekly brushing and infrequent baths. We bathe our dogs only if they have gotten muddy or have rolled in something unsavory during our hikes and bathe them before a show. It is amazing how clean even the white Canaan Dogs stay; they need no more baths than the darker colored dogs.

Canaan Dogs with the proper coat for the breed have a dense undercoat that protects them from the cool air of desert nights and insulates them during hot days. The amount of this undercoat varies greatly, depending on climate and season of the year. Dogs living in colder climates grow significantly thicker coats in winter than dogs living in warmer areas. During peak shedding in spring and summer, brushing on a daily or every-other-day basis is recommended to keep loose fur from accumulating on the floors of your house. Most Canaan Dogs enjoy being brushed.

Canaan Dogs have tough nails that resist wear. Our domestic dogs must have their nails trimmed regularly, every six to eight weeks, and sometimes more often. Most do not enjoy this, so it is best to start when they are puppies. Even if the nails don't really need trimming, just taking off the tips or pretending to tip the nails is good practice. Wait until the puppy is a bit tired and relax him with a bit of massage. Take your time. Make nail trimming a fun experience by providing a treat immediately before and after each nail is clipped. Do one or just a few nails each time and try to quit before the puppy struggles. If the puppy learns that struggling prevents you from trimming nails, he may continue this ruse, and you will then need help every time you trim. On the other hand, if you pin the puppy down, the experience becomes unpleasant. Another problem with struggling is that it increases the chance that you will cut the quick of a nail (cut it too short) and then the dog will really not like the experience. Try to make the sessions short, fun, and not a big deal.

COMPANIONSHIP

Wolves, the ancestors of domestic dogs, live in packs and are very social. It was precisely because of this social organization that is so similar to our own that humans developed domesticated dogs from wolves to serve as companion animals. Canaan Dogs are happiest if they are full members of the family rather than relegated to the backyard. They bond strongly with their owners and are very affectionate with them. Although they are somewhat independent, they still need and enjoy the company of their pack—your family and household—and they need the stimulation that company provides them.

The Canaan Dog is the original wash-and-wear dog. Throughout most of the year, all he needs is a weekly brushing and an occasional bath. U-AGII Ch. Micah Haviv me Kansas, NA, TT, CGC, owned by Lee Boyd.

SOCIALIZATION

All dogs need proper socialization, but this is absolutely critical with Canaan Dogs. Because they are derived from pariah dogs, they are genetically pre-programmed to be suspicious of the unfamiliar. Unwary Canaan Dogs do not survive in the wild. With proper socialization, however, you will have a dog that you can take anywhere.

After the first few days of settling into your home, it is important to begin socializing your puppy. Until your puppy is properly immunized at three months of age, you need to keep him home to protect him from contagious diseases. Invite friends and family over to meet the new puppy. Make sure that they take off their shoes and wash their hands to avoid tracking disease into the house. Let them gently hold the puppy, pet him, and play with him, or let him play about their feet while they are visiting.

Once your puppy is properly immunized, take him everywhere you can and expose him to as many different situations as possible. Try to make these positive experiences by maintaining an upbeat attitude and forking over plenty of treats. Reward confidence and ignore shy behavior. Don't reassure a pup when he is being shy, or the puppy will interpret this as praise for reacting with shyness. Show your pup with your relaxed and confident demeanor that the situation is perfectly normal; the pup will pick up his clues from you. Don't rush—a good practice is to let your puppy stay in a new environment for at least an hour or until he is completely comfortable.

The more places you take the pup and the more positive experiences he has, the better. Try to socialize

Signing up for a training class is a great way to socialize your dog. Once your Canaan masters various skills, he can participate in exciting events, like these Canaan Dogs at a National Specialty.

Although they are independent, Canaan Dogs are happiest if they are full members of the family and part of household life. AKC/ICDCA/CDCA Ch. Bay Path's Cherrysh My Delight, owned by the Hennings family.

the dog to everything you can think of. You may not have children now, but what about later? What if relatives or friends with children come for a visit? The pup should be exposed to children of different ages; dogs don't always generalize between infants, toddlers, or teenagers if they haven't met that age group previously. You may have to "hire" the children in your neighborhood to come play with the puppy, and you should remain on hand to supervise. This is a good way to enlist future dog-sitters and dog-walkers and build goodwill toward your dog among the children of the neighborhood.

You may not have cats now, but what about later? What if you want to leave your dog with friends while you take some vacation and they have cats? Find a friend with dog-savvy cats and let your puppy get acquainted.

Canaan Dogs are very territorial and as your puppy gets older, he will regard your home as the territory of his pack, your family, and start to bark at intruders. It is important that you expose the puppy early and often to people coming to your home so that having guests will become a normal event. A good method for introducing an older puppy or an adult dog to unfamiliar guests is to put the dog in another room or in his crate until the guests are in and seated. Then give the guests some treats and ask them to ignore the dog unless the dog approaches and seeks attention, in which case they are to reward him with a treat. If there is more than one dog, let out the most gregarious dog first; his confident behavior will reassure the shyer dogs. If a dog won't approach on his own, put him on a

25

leash after awhile and gently take him near where the guests are seated. The guests can drop treats on the floor for the dog to find. Once Canaan Dogs know the guests, they may let out a few alerting barks the next time they approach the house, but after they are inside and recognized, the dogs will be delighted to see them again. In fact, one of the things we like most about the breed is that they are devoted to friends and family and greet them affectionately without clinging.

It is also very important to socialize your puppy with other dogs, especially if you don't have other dogs at home. In nature, pups would learn proper dog etiquette from their littermates and from adults in the pack starting at about eight weeks of age. You have to provide them with a substitute for this experience. After the pup is three months of age, enroll him in a good puppy kindergarten class as soon as you can.

Local kennel clubs or veterinarians may offer puppy kindergarten classes. A good puppy kindergarten is one that allows time for free play among the puppies so that they encounter other breeds and learn social skills, such as inhibiting the strength of their bite. A good puppy kindergarten will also teach you basic training skills and help teach your dog basic manners such as sit, down, come, and stay on command. You might also discuss basic dog care if many first-time owners are in the class. If you can't find a puppy kindergarten in your area, your vet may be able to give you some names of people with similarly aged pups, and you can meet in your homes or a park to socialize the puppies.

After puppy kindergarten, especially if you have an "only" dog, try to find your pup at least one steady dog friend with whom he can play and interact regularly in order to maintain social skills. Keep the dogs under supervision but let them sort out their squabbles, intervening only if there is bloodshed. Pups that learn how to work out their differences at this stage are much less likely to overreact to other dogs when they grow up. If your pup tends to be somewhat dominant, pairing him with an older, larger dog willing to tolerate some but not all of his antics will provide the puppy with some needed discipline.

When the puppy is older, continue to take him to obedience classes or any other activity that involves training and provides exposure to new situations and new people. Socialization is an ongoing process, but all of this effort is worthwhile. A well-socialized Canaan Dog can adjust to almost anything.

SELECTING YOUR CANAAN DOG

Owning a Canaan Dog can enrich your life, but owning a dog takes work and responsibility. Dogs are not stuffed toys. They need basic care, walks, informal interaction, training, and supervision. They create all sorts of messes that you'll have to clean up. You must be certain you are ready to commit to dog ownership. You are essentially selecting a family member who will be with you for the next 15 years, so do not undertake the selection of a dog lightly and do your research carefully.

ARE CANAAN DOGS THE RIGHT BREED FOR YOU?

One of the purposes of this book is to help you decide whether this breed is suitable for you. In a nutshell, the pluses of Canaan Dogs are that they:
- are intelligent;
- are versatile;
- are agile and athletic;
- are healthy;
- are long-lived;
- are a very natural breed;
- have plenty of stamina yet need only moderate exercise;
- require little grooming;
- are self-reliant yet affectionate;
- are good with children (when socialized with them);
- are natural guardians without undue aggression;
- are the dog of the Bible and Holy Land; the only Israeli breed.

On the other hand, they:
• need an owner firmly in charge;
• can be dog aggressive;
• require extensive socialization to mitigate against their natural mistrust of strangers;
• are independent enough to require a fenced yard;
• bark persistently when defending their property from real or imagined intruders;
• shed.

Overall, they may not be the ideal choice for first-time dog owners.

Once you have decided to buy a Canaan Dog, you must give some thought as to whether to buy a pet- or show-quality dog, a male or a female, a puppy or an adult. Then you will need to locate and contact breeders.

COMPANION OR SHOW DOG?

If you want to breed your dog or show him in the breed ring, the choice is clear. You need a show dog. Sometimes people who start out just wanting a pet get hooked on showing. That happened to both of the

The decision to get a Canaan Dog should result from careful research and planning. You are essentially selecting a family member that will be with you for possibly the next 15 years. Keesha, owned by Kathy and Michael Bogner.

authors of this book! If your first dog is not of show quality, you may have to purchase a second dog in order to be competitive in the conformation ring. If you are really sure you just want a pet, or a second dog is not out of the realm of possibility if you find yourself getting drawn into showing, then by all means buy a pet-quality puppy to begin with. Pet-quality pups are slightly less expensive and may require a shorter wait. Find out why the breeder considers this to be a pet-quality dog. Maybe he is a bit too small or too large, has an improper coat color or pattern, or his ears are not erect. Maybe his movement is not as beautiful as it could be. All of these pet-quality dogs can make wonderful companions; however, they must be spayed or neutered so that they won't pass on their imperfections.

MALE OR FEMALE?

Which gender to choose is a matter of personal preference. If you already have another dog, especially if you don't plan to spay or neuter your Canaan Dog, it is safer to get a member of the opposite sex to lessen the chance of serious fighting. Regardless of which gender you purchase, have your pet neutered, unless it is a show-quality dog that you intend to show or breed. Generally, neutered pets have fewer behavior problems and health problems, and there is no risk of adding to the pet overpopulation problem. Moreover, they can compete in the US in any activity, except the breed ring. They are welcome in obedience, agility, tracking, flyball, and herding events, for example. If you'd like an occasional taste of the breed ring, the ICDCA offers classes for spayed and neutered dogs at its annual National Specialty, because we want all attendees to be able to participate if they desire and have fun showing off their beloved companion.

PUPPY OR ADULT?

Watching a puppy grow and mature is a very enjoyable and memorable experience. You have the opportunity to mold a puppy's behavior and to bring him up in the best way to fit into your family. However, taking care of a puppy can be a lot of work. Puppies require your time, energy, and patience if you are to raise them properly. They require a lot of socialization and create a lot of mess until completely housetrained and past the destructive stage.

Perhaps you don't have time to raise a puppy or would like to rescue an older dog. One advantage of an older dog is that he may already be housetrained and somewhat obedience trained, although dogs that have been kept in a kennel may be neither. Another advantage of an older dog is that "what you see is what you get." You know what the dog looks like and what his temperament is like. Find out why the dog has to be rehomed and how much socialization he has had. A properly socialized adult with no health or temperament problems can often adapt quickly to a new household. However, if the dog's early socialization was neglected or if the dog has temperament or health problems, it may now be more difficult to introduce the dog at this age to new environments and new stimuli such as cats and kids. We have known it to take almost a year for some older Canaan Dogs that have spent their life in a kennel to really integrate into their new family and surroundings. Canaan Dogs are not generally a breed for first-time dog owners, and this is particularly true of inadequately socialized older dogs. Their rescue is best left to those with a lot of dog experience who know how to handle the dog's disposition and ideally have some experience with this or similar breeds.

LOCATING A BREEDER

Fortunately, Canaan Dogs are not presently sold in pet stores, and we hope it stays that way. Most puppies that are sold in pet shops are usually born in squalor in puppy mills, receiving neither adequate care nor socialization. We recommend that the best course of action is to always buy a dog from a reputable private breeder.

There are relatively few breeders of Canaan Dogs, and there is some competition for puppy sales in addition to competition in the show ring. When talking with breeders, it is important to recognize hearsay and innuendo and take what is said about others with a grain of salt. If a breeder conducts himself or herself professionally, there is every expectation that they will treat you honorably as well.

The Israel Canaan Dog Club of America maintains a list of members who are breeders on its web site (www.itb.it/canaan/icdca) and has links to sites with lists of nonmember breeders. While listing does not constitute an endorsement of these breeders, they all care enough about the breed to belong to the club and abide by its code of ethics, which is also posted on the web site. If one of these breeders has no puppies available, they will usually refer you to another breeder who does.

When you contact breeders, you should feel as if they are interviewing you. Indeed, they are. They want to make sure that you are a suitable dog owner, that this breed is right for you, and that you have the commitment and the wherewithal to care properly for one of their dogs. Good breeders will tell you about the breed, both its good and bad points.

Similarly, you should be interviewing the breeder. Find out about the breeder's experience with dogs in general and with Canaan Dogs in particular. Is the breeder active and successful in conformation shows or in performance events? Does the breeder belong to a national Canaan Dog club? How many litters does the breeder produce per year? Does he raise any other breeds? It is possible for Canaan Dog breeders to be involved in another breed or to raise several litters in a year, but only someone with a lot of time and/or good hired help can have many dogs and still provide them with adequate attention. You, as a new puppy owner, may not receive adequate support and advice from a breeder who is too busy.

Ask for pedigrees of the sire and dam whose litter you are considering. Preferably, you will see titles on many of the ancestors. Even if you have no interest in showing, titles indicate some important characteristics. In order to be shown, a dog is subjected to many stressful situations during training and traveling to shows. He has performed well around strangers in strange settings, in the presence of unfamiliar dogs. For any dog to go through these experiences and win honors speaks volumes about the temperament and physical superiority of the dog.

Before deciding on a puppy or an adult, you must consider your family's needs and level of experience with dogs.

Keep in mind that there is a relatively small number of breeding-quality Canaan Dogs. Therefore, you might see some of the same relatives appearing in the grandparent and great-grandparent sides of the sire and dam of your puppy. However, close matings, fathers to daughters for example, are uncommon and should be avoided.

Do not buy a puppy whose parents have not been screened for genetic disease. Screening for hip dysplasia is essential, and eye and thyroid screening is desirable. This does not provide a guarantee that your puppy will be free of genetic defects, but you can improve the odds greatly by only accepting puppies from parents that have passed evaluations. Do not buy an adult dog without proof that he has been screened.

Breeding and raising quality dogs is expensive. Dedicated breeders must pay for extensive health screening and registration of their stock, pay stud fees and vet bills, buy premium dog food, pay entry fees, and travel to shows to exhibit their dogs. Breeders rarely make a profit on their litters. If you find a bargain dog, make sure you know exactly why he is such a bargain.

When possible, visit breeders in order to meet their dogs and to assess the conditions they are raised in. If they are a great distance from you, you might arrange to meet at a dog show if there is one closer to you that the breeder will be attending. The best place to meet breeders and their dogs is to attend the annual National Specialty, which is held in a different part of the country each year. There you can compare dogs, observe what each breeder is producing, and come to know the breeders a bit better. Especially if you intend to breed and show Canaan Dogs, we strongly recommend attending a specialty before purchasing your dog.

Often, the breeder whose dogs you most admire will not live near you, but puppies can safely be flown to you, even from overseas. Ideally, if you can find someone traveling from the breeder's city to yours, the pup can accompany that person in a crate at a much cheaper rate than if flown by freight. The minimum age at which domestic flights will accept pups is eight weeks, which is precisely the minimum age at which to obtain a pup, whether driving or flying. The minimum age for international travel is generally three months. International flights are not that much more expensive, especially if someone can be found to accompany the dog, and lower prices overseas may offset some of the cost of the flight. Arrangements are easily made by telephone, fax, or e-mail. Canaan Dog puppies have been flown to the US from Israel, Italy, and England. Particularly if you intend to breed, expanding the US Canaan Dog gene pool through importation is welcome.

Once you find a breeder whom you trust and whose dogs you like, be prepared to wait. This is a rare breed and reputable breeders breed very deliberately. A wait of almost a year to get a pup from a breeder whose dogs you admire is not unusual. The most common mistake people make is to be in a hurry to get a dog. We receive calls all the time from someone who wants a black male puppy two weeks from today. This is usually impossible and an indication of how little the caller has considered their decision. Anticipation is half the fun of getting a new puppy. Use the time to read up on the breed, read training books, join the national breed club, locate a good vet and training classes, mull over names, gather supplies, and puppy-proof your house and yard. Dust off your camera and buy film to record your puppy's milestones.

When the litter is born, you may or may not have your choice of puppies, depending on the litter size and composition and how stringent your requirements are for a particular sex or color. If you do have a choice and can visit the breeder, you can conduct puppy temperament tests, many of which are described in dog training books, to help you in your decision. Just as human siblings are alike yet different, each puppy in a litter is a unique individual. For most people, temperament should be the prime decision-maker. Let the breeder help you based on your level of dog experience and home environment. Shy or bossy puppies are best left to experienced dog owners who have the knowledge necessary to bring out the best in these puppies.

Deciding which one of these cuties to take home is a tough choice! Let your breeder help you pick the puppy that best fits your lifestyle and personality. Nine-week old-Canaan puppies, bred by Terry Bagley.

YOUR PUPPY'S NEW HOME

PICKING UP YOUR PUP

Your puppy should be a minimum of eight weeks of age before you bring him home. It is best to have the basic items you will need to care for your puppy before the pup's arrival date. The breeder may supply some items with the puppy, such as a collar, so ask what will accompany the pup. At a minimum, you will need a leash, collar, water bowl, food bowl, and a crate with bedding.

If possible, arrange to pick up the puppy early in the day so that he can settle in at your home before bedtime. Some Canaan Dogs are prone to carsickness, so if you collect the pup by car and hold the pup in your lap, be sure to have towels along. Many Canaan Dogs outgrow this queasiness, so don't be too worried about what this first car trip bodes for future travels. Puppies, like human babies, don't thermoregulate well, so if it is a hot day, make sure there is plenty of fresh air entering the car, but don't let it become too drafty.

Before your Canaan puppy arrives at his new home, be sure to purchase the basic items he'll need and have a supply of the food he's been eating on hand. Ch. Geva's Karniela of Kansas, TT, CGC, owned by Lee Boyd and Lorraine Stephens.

If your journey is long, you will need to stop periodically to let the pup relieve himself. Do not let the puppy wander around too much where other dogs have been, because of the risk of contracting infectious diseases before the pup's immune system has matured. If your puppy has a bowel movement in a public area, be sure to clean it up. The easiest way to do this is to carry plastic bags with you. Place the bag over your hand, pick up the feces using the bag as a glove, and turn the bag inside out to contain the feces. Dispose of the bag in a trash receptacle. As a responsible dog owner, you will be doing this for the rest of the dog's life, whenever he is in a public place. Too many parks and school yards have banned dogs because irresponsible owners did not clean up after them. Be a good neighbor and clean up after your dog on neighborhood walks as well. When cleaning up your yard at home, a pooper scooper tool can make the chore easy.

On long trips or when the pup is flown to you, you will want to put him in a crate. Crates serve as the dog's den and are a wonderful way to confine destructive puppies for short periods of time. They also aid in housetraining. A puppy-sized crate is best for flying; otherwise buy one that will fit when he is an adult. Adult Canaan Dogs generally require a medium or large crate. A crate is also helpful if you have to spend the night in a motel. Be considerate of other guests and do not let the puppy cry all night. If he starts crying, let him snuggle next to you or to your hand. Provide comfort rather than yelling or smacking the pup, which will get your relationship off to a bad start. The puppy is probably just lonely on his first night away from his mother and siblings.

After you arrive home and the puppy has explored his new surroundings, offer a light meal of food and water. Don't overfeed him, or the puppy may become sick after all the excitement. He will likely soon become very sleepy. Take the puppy to his crate and let him rest undisturbed. Children should be taught not to bother sleeping dogs.

THE FIRST NIGHT

The first few nights away from his mother and siblings can be traumatic for a new puppy. The pup may be lonely and a bit cold without the warmth of littermates nearby. To help the puppy cope, there are several things you can do. Make sure his bed is not in

The first few nights away from his mother and littermates can be traumatic for a new puppy. Providing a soft toy that your Canaan can snuggle up to will make him feel safe and secure.

a drafty location. Some bedding to curl up in will help keep him warm. A ticking clock may mimic the sound of his siblings' heartbeats. A soft toy about the size of another sibling will give him something to snuggle next to. A dim nightlight would allow him to see until his surroundings become more familiar to him.

If your puppy whimpers in the night after you have arrived home, there are two things you should avoid. One is to chastise him, because he will not understand it, and the other is to comfort him every time he cries, because you are reinforcing the crying. The pup will learn that if he wants you to come, all he has to do is cry loudly! If you have provided all the above comforts, try to ignore the whimpering. The pup will soon settle down and go to sleep. Of course, you can take the puppy to bed with you to solve the problem, but unless this is to be a permanent privilege (not recommended), you are only postponing the problem. The separation anxiety is likely to worsen as the puppy gets older and has developed an expectation of sleeping with you. Some of us like to have our dogs sleep in the bedroom, but in their crates, rather than on our bed. Canaan Dogs are very hierarchy-oriented, and if you have a dog that wants to run for higher office, allowing him to share your bed encourages him to think of himself as your equal, if not your superior. This is not a problem with every Canaan Dog, but until you can assess your dog's personality, it is wise to establish proper etiquette early. Like children, Canaan Dogs need structure and rules to learn how to behave properly.

DANGERS IN THE HOME

You will need to puppy-proof your home, as you would for a human toddler. Think about potential sources of danger in advance and take measures to protect your puppy from them.

Open Fires

Make sure a screen protects your pup from being burned by sparks spit by coal or wood fires.

Electrical Wires

Puppies are little chewing machines and do not understand that electrical cords are off-limits and dangerous. Unplug electrical appliances that are not in use and wrap up the cord so that it is out of reach. There are unpalatable concoctions that can be smeared on the cords of appliances that must remain plugged in, and you can try to raise or conceal the cord so as to make it less noticeable.

Open Doors

All it takes is a door or gate that is left open, and your puppy can be out on the street in an instant. All family members and guests should be reminded to make sure doors and gates are securely latched after passing through them.

Open Windows or Balconies

Your pup must be protected from falling from high places. Make sure open windows are screened and that your pup cannot fit through railings on balconies, patios, or decks. You can tack netting or chicken wire to the inside of railings to prevent your puppy from getting through.

Your home and yard hold many potential dangers for a mischievous little Canaan pup—like an open gate or door—so think about these in advance and make sure he is protected from them.

Ponds or Pools

Like children, puppies can easily drown. Be sure any pool or pond is well covered or fenced so that there is no chance of the puppy falling in, and supervise the puppy carefully at times when the protection is removed.

Washers and Dryers

Puppies have been known to crawl into front-loading washers or dryers for a nap. Keep the doors to these appliances closed and check carefully before turning them on.

Small Children

Canaan Dogs that are raised with children are generally excellent with them, as are many Canaan Dogs with little experience of children. However, children under the age of five should never be left unsupervised with adult dogs or puppies. Children should be taught from the outset that the puppy is not a stuffed toy to be dragged about, pulled, and mauled. The puppy also needs a respite from children to sleep and relax. A dog only has a few ways of protecting himself from an obnoxious child. He can move away or try to hide, but once he's done this he has no other recourse than to bark, growl, or nip if the child persists. Anticipate problems before they happen and if you see your dog trying to retreat, intervene and stop the child. Again, Canaan Dogs are usually excellent with children, but it is unreasonable to expect them to tolerate something that you wouldn't put up with if it were directed at you.

Children need to be shown how to hold a puppy and how to safely pick him up so as not to hurt him. One hand should cradle the dog by passing under the dog's chest behind his forelegs. The other hand should cup the puppy's rump and hindlegs to lift him. Young children are too small to accomplish this and should not attempt to carry the puppy lest they drop him.

Beyond the dangers already cited, you may be able to think of others in your home, such as steep steps. Baby gates can be invaluable in keeping your puppy away from hazards and in a part of your home that is safe and puppy-proofed.

OTHER PETS

If you have decided to have two puppies or already have another pet, they will provide company for each other. If you have other pets, you will want to introduce your new puppy to them carefully with a lot of supervision. Canaan Dog puppies get along fine with any other pets, but you must keep in mind the respective size differences and the playful nature of puppies. A rowdy puppy can be a major aggravation to an older dog or cat. For the first couple of days, you might keep the puppy in another room from your older animals, and then switch them so that each can sniff where the other has been. Next, confine the puppy to a crate or behind a baby gate and let the older residents interact with him through the grating. Then you are ready to let the puppy out to interact, still with supervision. Praise good behavior and distract the participants if they are getting too rough. Respect your older animal's need for some quiet time and attention from you, away from the pesky pup. Older animals are often incredibly tolerant of a puppy's antics. However, as the puppy gets older, they will start to discipline him more. Unless there is bloodshed, you should not interfere. Your older animals are doing you a favor by helping bring up the puppy properly. They will teach him the social skills he needs to interact acceptably with other dogs, cats, etc.

Remember that if you do not have other animals but intend to some day, now is the time to introduce your puppy to members of these species. Find a friend with a cat that is used to dogs, for example, and let the puppy visit their house a couple of times. Afterward, cats will be no big deal.

HOUSETRAINING AND CRATING
Many books contain information about housetraining, and it would be wise to read up on this subject.

Crates have many uses such as confining puppies during their destructive phase. This crate is more than large enough for an adult Canaan Dog.

Although you should begin housetraining right away, puppies cannot control their bowels or bladder until they are about three months old and may be as old as six months of age before becoming completely reliable. You must be prepared for a few accidents, which you can minimize by anticipating the puppy's needs. Puppies typically urinate and defecate shortly after waking from a nap, shortly after eating, and after vigorous play. If you are alert, you may see the puppy circling with his nose to the floor looking for a suitable place. Quickly pick the puppy up and take him to the spot in your yard that you intend for him to use as a latrine. Stay with the puppy until he goes and praise him profusely. If he had an accident in the house, say nothing. Confine the puppy while you thoroughly clean the spot. Sites that have been used once will likely be used again, and dogs have a very keen nose, so clean the spot well. Watch the puppy more closely and make sure to take him outside promptly the next time and profusely praise any elimination that occurs outdoors. You might even give him a treat immediately after the act. To give these reinforcements you must be outside when the puppy eliminates. It is no use to praise the pup when he comes to the door to be let in; the puppy will just think you are praising him for entering the house. The puppy will soon learn that urinating and defecating outside is the only context in which he receives praise for these actions.

A crate can be a great adjunct for housetraining. Either a wire crate or a plastic airline kennel will do. Wire crates have the advantage of collapsing easily for transport, but if you think you will ever fly with your dog, get an airline-approved molded plastic crate, available from catalogs and many pet stores. As an adult, your Canaan Dog will need a medium- or large-sized crate. Ask your breeder how big they think your puppy will become when deciding which size to buy.

Dogs look upon crates as their dens, which they will not soil if at all possible. Put some bedding and safe toys in the crate. The door can be left open, so that the puppy can come and go. When you need to confine the pup or he is sleepy, put him in the crate and shut the door. The pup should not be left too long in the crate, and when he wakes up, you should take the puppy outside immediately to eliminate. If he does so, praise him. When he eliminates outside, you can reasonably assume that he can be loose in the house for awhile without accidents. If he fails to eliminate, put him back in the crate for a brief time and then try again.

Crates have many other wonderful uses. They can be used to confine puppies during destructive phases, although if you work outside the home, you will need to come home or have someone else stop by several times during the day to let the puppy out to eliminate. Crates give the dog a safe haven in which to sleep undisturbed, as they would in a den. Crates are essential for travel. They are required for airline travel, and will act like a child-safety restraint system in cars to keep the dog out of the driver's way and protected in case of an accident. Motels that won't accept dogs loose in the room may make exceptions if the dog can be crated. Crates can be used anywhere you have to leave your dog momentarily where a stay command won't suffice; at dog shows, in the car so the windows

If a puppy bites too hard, the victim will retaliate or leave, which puts an end to play thereby teaching the pup bite inhibition. This youngster is about to be disciplined for inappropriate behavior toward his elders.

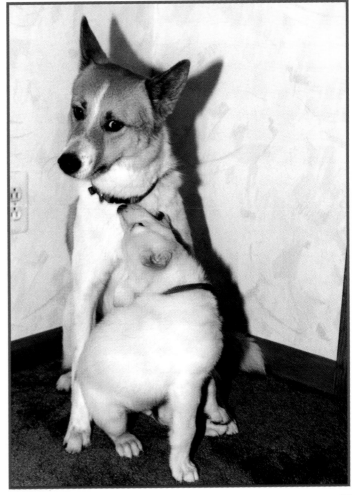

can be rolled down, etc. The bottom half of a large plastic crate also makes a great whelping box for pregnant bitches.

MOUTHING

Dogs use their mouths to explore and manipulate objects in their world, much as humans use their hands. Puppies have to learn how to use their mouth and teeth gently, without hurting people or other dogs and cats.

In nature, the learning process is simple. Puppies have needle-sharp teeth and when a playful puppy grabs a littermate and bites too hard, the other pup cries out and retaliates or goes away. In either case, this puts a stop to the play and teaches the biter that if he wants to continue playing, he must be more careful next time. These interactions teach bite inhibition or control of biting force, which will prevent dogs from drawing blood in all but the most dire disputes. Puppies that fail to learn control of their jaw pressure may deliver injuring bites as adults.

Owners can replicate the process by which bite inhibition is developed. When the puppy licks you gently, praise and pet him, saying, "gentle" or "easy." When you feel his teeth closing on your skin, yell, "Ouch!" loudly and move away from the puppy, as his offended littermate would. Wait awhile, and when you see that the pup is taken aback by the loss of your company and somewhat subdued, approach and resume gentle play.

If the puppy does not heed your cry and departure, but follows and continues to bite at you, it may be necessary to give the puppy a brief "time out" in his crate until he calms down. If the puppy still fails to get the message, you may need something more convincing. You might tap his open mouth with the flat of your hand, saying, "No bite." The tap should be light enough not to hurt the pup, but firm enough to catch his attention and block the mouthing movement.

A pup that consistently mouths too hard may benefit from interacting with an older or larger dog that can be relied upon not to hurt the puppy, but is assertive enough to discipline him for such inappropriate behavior.

IDENTIFICATION

Unfortunately, many dogs are stolen or lost every year. Your dog should be permanently identified with a microchip or tattoo, as well as wear a tag on his collar.

It is important that your dog wear a collar when he leaves the house, with a tag bearing your name, address, and phone number. Your community may require that your dog be licensed, and the license tag on the collar is another means of connecting the dog to you if found. Your dog should also wear his rabies tag, which provides yet another way to match a lost dog to his owner. You should use a leather or nylon collar to bear the tags. Never use a choke collar, also called a training collar, as your dog's permanent collar. These collars are dangerous to leave on an unsupervised dog. One of the rings may catch on something and the dog could be strangled if he panics. During training, this type of collar is placed on the dog by sliding it on and off over the ears. It can easily slide right off by itself, leaving the dog with no identification tags at all.

In fact, in case the collar is lost or removed, your dog should also bear some permanent identification. Tattoos are one form of permanent identification. The dog can be tattooed with a registration number that is recorded by a national organization that can be contacted if someone finds the dog. Tattoos are most commonly placed on the inner side of one of the dog's upper hindlegs or inside the ear. Another form of permanent identification is the microchip. This little computer chip is about the size of a grain of rice and can be injected under the skin of the dog's shoulder. It bears a number that can be read with a scanner. The number is registered with a national organization. Most veterinarians and animal shelters now have scanners and are probably more likely to check incoming dogs for microchips than tattoos. They will call the registering organization to report the scanned number and obtain the information on how to contact you.

Getting accustomed to a new environment may be difficult for a young puppy or an adopted older dog. Care, kindness, and encouragement will make your pet feel confident and help him to become a well-adjusted companion. Cherrysh my Noblis Aljan, owned by Caren Curtiss.

FEEDING YOUR CANAAN DOG

Today's dog owners are fortunate to live in an age when considerable resources have been invested in studying canine nutritional needs. Dog food manufacturers are very concerned about ensuring that their foods are of the best quality. The number of products is unlimited, so it is hardly surprising that dogs generally suffer from obesity and vitamin excess, rather than the reverse. A dry kibble diet is recommended, as it is cheaper than canned food and better for the health of your dog's teeth. Canned food is tastier and can be added to the diet on those occasions when you are struggling to put some additional weight on your dog. Canned food is also useful for disguising medications you want your dog to ingest.

Be sure to feed an age-appropriate food. Generally, a diet formulated for puppies should be fed the first year, followed by adult food up to seven or eight years of age, when a senior diet should be fed. You should almost always feed smaller quantities than the manufacturer recommends, or else your Canaan Dog will become obese.

FACTORS AFFECTING NUTRITIONAL NEEDS
Activity Level
A dog that lives in a country environment and is able to exercise for long periods of time will need more food than he would in an apartment with exercise limited to on-lead walks.

Quality of the Food
Obviously, the quality of the food will affect the quantity required by a puppy. If the nutritional content of a food is low, then the puppy will need more of it than if a better quality food was fed.

44

Balance of the Nutrients and Vitamins

Feeding a puppy the correct balance of nutrients is not easy, because the average person is not able to measure out ratios. A good-quality prepared puppy food takes the guesswork out of feeding.

Genetic and Biological Variation

Apart from all other considerations, it should be remembered that each puppy is an individual. His genetic makeup will influence not only his physical appearance, but also his metabolic efficiency. This being so, two pups from the same litter can vary quite a bit in the amount of food they need in order to perform the same activities under the same conditions. If you consider the potential combinations of all these factors, then you will see that pups of a given breed could vary quite a bit in the amount of food they will need. Before discussing amounts to feed, it is valuable to know at least a little bit about the composition of food and its role in the body.

For the first few weeks of life, a baby Canaan Dog's mother supplies all of the nutrition he requires. After that, it becomes your responsibility to feed your dog a healthy, well-balanced diet that includes the proper amount of proteins, fats, and carbohydrates. Hila me Shaar Hagai with her litter, owned by Christine and David Franklin.

COMPOSITION AND ROLE OF FOOD

The main ingredients of food are proteins, fats, and carbohydrates, each of which is needed in relatively large quantities when compared to vitamins and minerals. The other vital ingredient of food is, of course, water. Although all foods obviously contain some of the basic ingredients needed for an animal to survive, they do not

Always be sure to feed age-appropriate food designed to meet the nutritional needs of your puppy, adult, or senior dog. AKC/CDCA Ch. Cherrysh Gideon's Topaz CGC, owned by Jerry and Cheryl Hennings.

all contain these ingredients in the proper ratio or form. For example, there are many forms of protein, just as there are many types of carbohydrates. Both of these compounds are found in meats and vegetables—but not all of those that are needed will be found in one particular meat or vegetable. Plants, in particular, do not contain certain amino acids that are required for the synthesis of certain proteins needed by dogs.

Likewise, vitamins are found in meats and vegetable matter, but vegetables are the richer source of most vitamins. Some vitamins can be synthesized by the dog, and so do not need to be supplied via the food. During the preparation process, the vitamin content is either greatly reduced or lost altogether. The manufacturer therefore adds vitamins once the heat process has been completed, making sure that all the vitamin needs of dogs are satisfied in a balanced way. This is why commercial foods are so useful as part of a feeding regimen, provided that they are of good quality and from a company that has prepared the foods very carefully.

An excess of vitamins, especially A and D, has been proven to be harmful. Provided a puppy is receiving a balanced diet, it is most unlikely there will be a deficiency, whereas hypervitaminosis (an excess of vitamins) has become quite common due to owners and breeders feeding unneeded supplements. The only time you should feed extra vitamins to your puppy is if your veterinarian advises you do so.

Minerals provide strength to tissues as well as assist in many metabolic processes. They are essential to nerve and muscle function and blood formation and clotting. Examples of important minerals are calcium, phosphorous, copper, iron, magnesium, selenium, potassium, zinc, and sodium. Calcium and phosphorous are important to puppies in forming bones during growth. However, as with vitamins, a mineral deficiency is most unlikely in pups fed a commercial balanced diet, and an excess can create problems. This applies to calcium and phosphorous as well. Unless your veterinarian advises it, do not feed supplemental minerals.

Water is the most important of all ingredients. This is easily shown by the fact that the adult dog is made up of about 60 percent water, and puppies contain an even higher percentage. Dogs must maintain a water balance, which means that the total intake should be balanced by the total output. The intake comes both through drinking and metabolic water released when food is oxidized. A dog without adequate water will lose condition more rapidly than one without adequate food,

The amount of exercise your Canaan Dog receives affects his food intake. A very active dog will require more to eat than a less active dog of the same size.

Establishing a feeding schedule with set amounts of food will help you to monitor your Canaan's overall health. Carocane Fatima, owned by Sari Alanko, Finland.

a fact common to most animal species. In general, dogs should have clean, fresh water available to them at all times.

AMOUNT TO FEED

The best way to determine dietary requirements is by observing the puppy's general health and physical appearance. If he is well covered with flesh, shows good bone development and muscle, and is an alert, active puppy, then the diet is probably adequate. You should ask the breeder of your puppy to tell you the amounts fed to their pups and this will be a good starting point. As an adult, your dog is too thin if the ribs are clearly visible and too fat if you cannot feel the ribs easily under your hands.

The puppy should eat his meal in about five to ten minutes. Any leftover food can be discarded or placed into the refrigerator until the next meal (but be sure to let it warm a bit before feeding).

If the puppy is not overweight, quickly devours his meal, and is clearly still hungry, then you are not giving him enough food. If he eats readily but then begins to pick at the remainder or leaves the rest, then you are probably giving him too much food. Begin to adjust this at the next meal. If, over a number of weeks, the puppy starts to look fat, then he is overeating and you should lessen the amount given. The reverse is true if the puppy starts to look thin. Worm infestations can cause loss of weight, so you might also want to speak with your veterinarian about checking for internal parasites.

If adults become overweight and cutting back on their food makes them ravenous, increase their daily exercise and feed a diet formulated for overweight dogs that provides filling bulk with fewer calories.

Feeding tidbits to dogs at the table is not advisable as it can lead to annoying begging behavior. Also, some "human foods" are bad for your dog. Chocolate can be lethal. Make sure guests are aware of this and store all chocolate out of the dog's reach. Do not feed cooked bones to dogs because they splinter. Raw bones, even chicken bones, are safer.

WHEN TO FEED

Puppies from 8 weeks to 16 weeks of age need 3 or 4 meals a day. Older puppies should be fed twice a day, and many owners continue this into adulthood. Some owners feed their adult dogs only once daily. Dogs appreciate routine, and their feeding times should be reasonably regular. This can be tailored to fit with your own schedule—for example, 7 am and 6 pm. Keeping regular feeding times and feeding set amounts will help you monitor your dog's health. If a dog that is normally enthusiastic about mealtimes suddenly shows a lack of interest, you'll know that something is not right.

Puppies from 8 to 16 weeks of age need to be fed 3 or 4 meals a day. Older puppies should be fed twice a day and many owners continue this into their dog's adulthood. Canaan puppies owned by Ian and Jill Terry, England.

TRAINING YOUR CANAAN DOG

Start training your pup from the moment he enters your home. Your pup will be learning something whether you formally teach it or not—he might as well learn what you'd like him to know.

The key to training any dog, especially Canaan Dogs, is to create a good rapport between owner and dog. Your pet must trust you and must respect you, and he must, of course, accept you as the "leader of the pack."

Canaan Dogs have not been bred to work for humans. As much as they may love their owner, by and large they will not translate their love into an unqualified willingness to please. They are intelligent, independent animals. Time after time, they will look at you with a sparkle in their eye and tell you, "Okay, I understand what you want. But give me a good reason to do it." It is your task to present them with that good reason.

Most of the time, your answer will be through positive reinforcement, using something that your dog really likes. Some Canaan Dogs are "chow hounds": They will be highly motivated by food. If yours is, count your

Start training your puppy as soon as he has settled into your home and responds to his name.

blessings—he will be much easier to train. If not, find as many other motivators as you can; praise, toys, or whatever else pleases your dog.

Combined with positive reinforcement, you will eventually need to add some firmness. Your dog will one day tell you, "I don't feel like eating another treat right now, I'll come back to play or work with you later." Then you must consistently remind him that he does not have that choice.

With dogs as intelligent as Canaan Dogs, you have to be very careful not to give them any command, even as puppies, which they are in a position to ignore. They have excellent hearing—repeating a command just teaches them to obey you only at the second or third time or when you start shouting. This holds true in a formal training session, but even more so in your day-to-day interactions with your dog.

There are a few basic commands that you'll need to teach your pup early on. As pups have a short attention span and not as much stamina as older dogs, it is better if you keep your lessons to five to ten minutes long. Better to have two or three positive, very short sessions daily rather than a single long session that is too demanding.

The best choice is first to combine training at home with a puppy kindergarten class and then with beginners training classes, starting as soon as possible after your pup has his shots at three months of age. Group classes offer an invaluable source of socialization and exposure to new situations, people, and dogs, and, of course, they should provide the hands-on assistance of an experienced trainer.

When you are training at home, choose a moment when you are more likely to have the full attention of your pup. Train when your pup is rested and eager to get some stimulation and attention from you, such as soon after you take him from his crate. That way he associates working with you with fun and stimulation. Always end your session on an upbeat note, praising and rewarding your pup for something done right.

COLLAR AND LEASH TRAINING

Your pup may have already come from the breeder with a collar, and perhaps he has already had some experience with a leash. But if he has not, without making much fuss, put a collar on him. We recommend a flat buckle collar in leather or nylon. When your pup is older, you may want to try a training collar, but with a puppy it may be excessive. You will also need a five- or six-foot nylon or leather leash.

Your pup may initially try to scratch the collar or run away from it, but will soon come to ignore it, especially if you distract the puppy by playing with him or feeding him. You may leave the collar on him for a few hours and then each day increase the length of time. If the puppy doesn't initially object to the collar, leave it on, although it is not advisable to leave a collar on a very young unsupervised pup as accidents can occur all too easily. Check the collar regularly as the puppy grows to make sure it is not becoming too tight or irritating the skin. If you are concerned that the collar will mar the dog's coat, you can take the collar off when the dog is safely indoors for the night.

Once the puppy completely ignores the collar, attach the leash and let the pup drag it around for a few minutes, but don't let the puppy chew on it on and be ready to free the pup if the leash catches on some obstacle. Repeat a few times a day, until the pup ignores the leash also.

Next, take the leash in your hand and walk with the pup. At some stage, he will discover that the leash restricts his movements and he may put up a fuss by pulling back, biting the leash, etc. Distract him and attract him to you; give him a treat, a toy, make noises, whatever is necessary to make him forget his sudden lack of freedom and make being close to you more appealing. Take care that the first associations with the leash are pleasant.

THE SIT COMMAND

Whenever you are around the house and see your pup about to sit on his own, say, "Rover, sit," and praise him. He will start to vaguely associate your word with his action. After several such instances, you can introduce this command in a regular training session.

Teaching your puppy to sit is very easy if you have a food-motivated dog. When he is standing close to you on your left side, take his collar in your left hand and bring a treat toward his nose, passing it low over the pup's head but just out of reach, saying, "Rover, sit," as you do so. Holding the collar will keep the puppy from turning, backing up, or jumping up. In order to keep his eyes on the treat, the puppy will raise his head and rock back on his haunches into a sit. The instant his rump touches the ground, praise the puppy lavishly and give him the treat. After several sessions, you'll be able to stand erect with the treat in sight and have the puppy sit at your command in expectation of the treat. Then practice with the treats out of sight in your pocket, only presenting them after the puppy obeys the sit command.

If your pup is less food-motivated or is distracted, some physical positioning will be necessary. When he is standing close to you on your left side, put your right hand on his chest and your left hand on his rump. Then say, "Rover, sit," push back with your right hand, and hold or push slightly down and toward the front with your left hand. The puppy will find himself sitting on his rump. Praise him lavishly. In just a few days, your puppy will get the hang of it and will start anticipating your positioning. Praise and reward his cooperation and start reducing your physical help, ready to reintroduce it quickly the first time the puppy does not react to your command.

A young pup's joints are immature, and you should be careful not to push too hard on his rump. If you find yourself pushing hard, try positioning your left hand behind the pup's rump instead. Remember that most of the positioning action is achieved by the correct movement of your right hand on the pup's chest, not of the left one. When your older dog needs a reminder on the sit command, you can pull slightly up and back on his leash instead of pushing on his chest.

THE HEEL COMMAND

When your pup is completely used to the leash and doesn't fight it, you may use the leash itself to control the puppy's movements. First, never drag the pup or tow him with the leash. This just urges him to pull in the opposite direction. It is important that you teach him that he

Your Canaan Dog must learn to accept a collar and leash for his safety and the safety of others in order that he may accompany you. Dune, owned by Caren Curtiss.

Bay Path's Jersey Girl Tasha, CGC, TDI, owned by Michael and Kathy Bogner, performs the perfect sit/stay.

doesn't achieve anything by pulling. If he starts pulling, say, "Don't pull," and stop moving until there is some slack in the leash. When you see that he understands this concept, you can start controlling his pulling also by jerking the leash. Use short jerks that are just strong enough to move the pup in the required direction, with an immediate release of the tension after the jerk. As soon as he moves under the effect of the leash, praise and reward him. This way he will associate moving close to you with something positive. At this stage, you will be able to take him on a short walk with a leash or a flexi-lead and have him go in your general direction.

The next step is to teach your pup the heel command. This is used when you want the puppy to walk really close to you without bumping into you. During the heel, he should be paying attention to you and adapting to your changes of pace and direction, so that you will be able to take him to more crowded areas, through traffic, etc., without having to constantly control him.

As with all new exercises, start this one when the puppy is attentive and not distracted. Place the puppy at your left side and ease him into a sit or tell him to sit if he already knows the sit command. Take the leash in your right hand and pass it through your left hand, leaving a little bit of slack. Attract his attention with a treat or a toy, say, "Rover, heel," and step forward with your left foot first. Chances are he will follow you, in which case you should praise him enthusiastically. If not, give him a light jerk with the leash—an attention-getter, not a correction. Attract him to move close to you. A treat or a toy held in your left hand in front of his nose will help.

You want the puppy to walk on your left, parallel to you, not touching you, but not more than six to nine inches from you, with his ear aligned to your left hip. Help him stay in that position by using short positioning jerks with your leash that are delicate enough not to scare him. Talk to him frequently and encourage him a lot. The first few times you try it, stop after he has made four or five steps in approximately the correct position. Praise him and reward him as if he had won the first prize in an obedience competition. The puppy will associate all the fuss you make with that fairly strange but not really unpleasant experience of having his natural movements controlled as to speed, position, and timing.

Then progressively lengthen your heeling stretch. Be picky about the puppy's position, because this is when he is learning where you want him; correcting mistakes later will be much harder. Gradually start reducing the fuss you make, but keep talking to the pup and engaging his attention. Introduce some gentle curves and encourage him to stay in heel position there, too. Change your pace a little by slowing down or speeding up and make him adapt his pace to you.

After you can tell that the puppy knows heel position, start making sharper turns and about turns. At the beginning, provide more help to build his experience and confidence. When you are sure the pup understands what is expected from him, if he moves intentionally out of heeling position, your jerk on the collar may turn into a mild reminder, "Hey, you are supposed to be with me, come back."

Don't heel him for more than a minute at a time. There will be plenty of time to practice precision heeling when the puppy is older, if you decide to engage in the sport of obedience. At this stage, the best you can do is to teach him three basic lessons: There is a position he is supposed to stay in when you heel; heeling is fun because he gets a lot of attention, fuss, and treats; and heeling (like other work) is something that has to be done properly. He is not given a choice.

Aside from having practical uses, the stay command teaches your dog self-control. He should be able to remain in position until you release him, as this obedient Canaan demonstrates with a down/stay. Jazz me Shaar Hagai, owned by Myrna Shiboleth, Israel. Photo by Yigal Pardo.

THE STAY COMMAND

You teach this command only after your pup knows the sit. Place him in a sit on leash at your left side, say, "Rover, stay," and wait 10 to 20 seconds. If he tries to get up, stop him without making much fuss about it. Pulling upward on the leash will often cause the dog to sit again. For the stay command, you will need to give a release command, such as "Free," and then playfully encourage the puppy to get up. After the pup understands that he is not supposed to move after you command him to stay, start pivoting in front of him. Again, if he moves, stop him gently with the leash and reposition him in his sit without saying anything. Next, try circling around him in order to return to heel position on his right and praise him. Very gradually, increase the time and the distance you are away from him.

If the puppy still breaks the sit after he really understands the command, for instance by going into a down, reposition him a little less gently to make him understand that this is not acceptable. By the time your pup is an adult, he should be able to stay for up to five minutes with you out of sight, but it is much better not to rush this exercise while the pup is young.

Once the puppy knows the stay during training, you should continue to practice it at home. You will find this command very handy, but you will have to teach the pup that "stay" in another situation means the same thing as it does during training. *Never* put a dog in a stay position and forget him there while you do something else, because this amounts to teaching him to disobey your commands, as he will surely get up of his own volition after awhile.

THE DOWN COMMAND

As with the sit command, you can get a head start on the down command by observing your pup around the house. Whenever you see your puppy about to lie down on his own, say, "Rover, down," and praise him. He will start to vaguely associate your word with his action.

If you have a food-motivated dog, the easiest method to teach the down is as follows: Have the dog sit at your left side. Bend over or kneel and put your left hand across the pup's back. With your right hand, bring a treat from the puppy's nose down toward the ground and forward a bit, saying "Rover, down." The puppy will naturally lower his nose to follow the treat, and with luck, will slide his forepaws out to get into a prone position to reach the treat. If he does so, praise him lavishly and give him the treat. The function of your left hand is to keep your pup from standing or pouncing on the treat.

If your pup is not food-motivated or if he does not slide his paws forward into a complete down, use your right hand under the forelegs to ease them forward. As soon as the chest touches the ground, praise the pup and make it clear that this is a positive, fun exercise and not a punishment. Steady him in the down position for a few seconds while praising him softly—if he doesn't struggle—and then release him.

This is a submissive position and shy pups may misunderstand your intention and try to show their complete submission by rolling over to expose their belly. Try to prevent them from rolling this far and use lots of encouragement to boost their confidence.

For the same reason, bolder pups may resist your command and struggle not to go down; they don't want to submit. If you coordinate your movements well and start teaching this command when the pup is young and you can control him better, he will have no choice. He will soon learn that this is a training exercise and not a one-upmanship on your part and will accept it. But his reaction to this exercise may give you useful early insight on his temperament and dominance level.

An alternative, harsher method used by many instructors to teach the down command is to jerk downward on the leash. We prefer to use this method only as a correction with somewhat older dogs that already know the command but do not obey it promptly.

THE COME COMMAND

This is the most important of all commands and may be a lifesaver, especially for a breed as independent as the Canaan Dog. It should be taught as soon as your pup recognizes his name and gets used to the leash. Put him on a long line or a flexi-lead and let him wander six to eight feet from you. When he is not too intent on something else, say, "Rover, come," and at the same time, give a slight jerk on the line. Crouch so as to be less threatening, make enticing sounds, show him a treat; whatever will bring him to you willingly. Retrieve the line without pulling if your pup comes, but give some additional slight jerks to make him come if your pup doesn't understand or doesn't comply. When the puppy reaches you, reward him both with praise and treats or petting. After a few times, when the pup realizes how nice it is to come to you, you can reduce the crouch and then eliminate it completely. When the puppy comes to you, ease him into a sit in front of you before you give him a treat or pet him.

There are two key points in this exercise. The first is that you want to leave your pup *absolutely no choice* as to whether to comply promptly or not. That's why the light jerk on the line must come together with your command, not after it. This will make the dog come more automatically, reducing any hesitations after the command. The dog should not be left time to ponder whether or not to obey. You must carefully calibrate the jerk itself. Initially, it ought to be just an attention-getter. If you see that your pup needs more guidance, the jerk should still be delicate but longer to help bring him toward you. If you see that your pup comes willingly, the jerk can be very light indeed. Later on, when you are sure that your pup really understands the command and you see him slowing down, ambling in another direction, or just refusing to come, the jerk on the line can turn into something more directive like, "Hey guy, I told you to come here, *right now*."

The second point is to make the outcome of the command *always* pleasant or at least neutral. Never scold your pup after using the come command or use it to call your pup for some unpleasant activity such as nail clipping, etc. For these purposes, quietly approach your pup and take him where you want him, but do not call him to you.

Also, do not make the common mistake of testing the come command when you are not in a position to physically enforce its prompt execution until your pup is fully trained and you are sure you can rely on his recall. Once your pup learns that when the lead is off he can easily outrun you, months of good work will be undone. So, if your pup is free in the yard and you want him to approach you, call him or entice him by using different words.

When you think your pup's recall is reliable, the best place to test your come command off leash is in a closed room or a very small, fenced area. If your pup doesn't promptly come, do not call him again. Quietly walk to where he is, take him with both hands by the collar, and back off up to the place you were when you gave him the command. In other words, make him execute the come. Then put your pup back on leash for at least a few more weeks.

With training, there are no limits to what your Canaan Dog can do. U-UD Ch. Lahatut me Shaar Hagai, UD CKC-CDX, TT, owned by Victor Kaftal.

CANINE BEHAVIOR AND TEMPERAMENT

DOMINANCE

In a wolf or dog pack, it is the alpha dog and alpha bitch that lead the pack, maintain order, procreate, and pass their genes to future generations. This high rank is definitely coveted by wild dogs. As a primitive, natural breed, Canaan Dogs are more concerned with their position in the pack hierarchy than more derived breeds. Dominant Canaan Dogs (or bitches) make confident, self-assured, wonderful companions that can more easily be taken to new places and adapt

Like their ancestors the wolves, dogs are social creatures that live in an extended family pack. It is important to establish yourself as the pack leader from the beginning of your relationship with your Canaan Dog.

This puppy is challenging an older dog for possession of his chew stick. Dogs show dominance by taking a higher position, mounting, or putting a muzzle or stiff paw on you. Niki and Ryder, owned by Katryna Bogovich.

more quickly to new situations. But they need owners who are firmly in charge.

In nature, it is normal for a dominant adolescent to try to challenge the leaders of his pack in order to test if they are past their prime. But alpha dogs do not tolerate alpha behavior in subordinate dogs; uppity underlings are promptly put in their place. If the alpha is old or sick and repeatedly ignores the challenges, the youngster will eventually make a move to take his (or her) place and a fight will occur. If the same happens at home, you may have serious trouble, because it is your or your family members' place that the budding leader is trying to occupy. As you are not a dog, you may not even be aware of having been challenged until very late in the game. Dominance problems are one of the serious causes of incompatibility between Canaan Dogs and their owners.

The signals that indicate that your dog is running for higher office in your pack can sometimes be subtle. When you are sitting or lying down, does your dog try to climb higher than you? Does he often approach you strutting a bit, his ears up and pointed forward? Does he try to mount your leg or put a stiff paw on you? Does he rush through thresholds before you? Does he studiously ignore some of your orders as if he didn't hear? Does he physically resist some of your handling? While it may be cute in pups, mouthing in adolescent or adult dogs is often a serious precursor of biting. Mouthing of the leash is sometimes a substitute for mouthing of the hand that holds that leash and can be meant as a warning.

Sometimes the messages are more explicit but are still ignored by the owner. Some owners may say, "Oh, Rover is so possessive of his bone (favorite toy, armchair, food, etc.) that he doesn't let anyone touch it." Any growling at the owners should not be tolerated, and any biting whatsoever must be taken *very seriously* even if no real damage has (yet) been inflicted.

So, how do you react to such dominance displays? First, be aware of them. At the beginning stage, a dog is watching for any sign of opposition to his challenges and will back off easily.

Second, work proactively on your relationship with your dog. Start in puppyhood and continue through adolescence, at a minimum. In the case of very dominant dogs, you may need to keep this up for years. The following are helpful practices with all pups and can be applied more often and more intensively with a more confident pup. If your adolescent dog is already showing some signs of dominance, you may want to introduce these exercises cautiously and gradually, to avoid triggering an active rebellion—unless you are prepared and willing to deal with it.

Don't let your dog precede you through doors or up the stairs. Occasionally make him sit before doors and then let him cross through them only with your permission.

Make your dog wait for permission to get his food when you lay it down. Put him on leash if necessary, make him stay, put the dish in front of him, make him wait at least 10 to 30 seconds, then give him permission and let him eat. Preferably, feed him after you have eaten, not before. In the pack, dominant dogs always eat first.

Occasionally interrupt his meal and make him sit (with some convincing, if necessary, from the leash) and wait for your permission to eat again. Give that permission promptly and praise him. Even if your dog is not possessive of his food, this exercise will impress on him that you have the power to give or withhold his food and that he has to obey you if he wants to eat; hence you must be higher up in the pack hierarchy.

After he accepts your stopping him when he eats without resentment, start picking up his bowl, make him wait a few seconds, and then put it back down again. Occasionally surprise him by adding a tastier morsel to the bowl before returning it. Next, try taking food out of his mouth, making him wait a few seconds

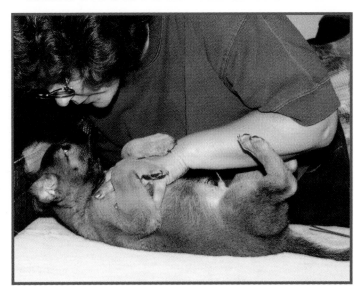

Putting a dog in a down position is an excellent diagnostic of the relationship between you and your dog. If he resists, he is not accepting your leadership without question. Cherrysh My Whale of a Time, owned by Jerry and Cheryl Hennings.

and then returning the food to him, occasionally supplying a tastier morsel instead. Besides helping with dominance, this exercise could be a lifesaver if he picks up something he shouldn't eat from the ground. Do the same with bones, toys, etc.

Dogs show dominance by taking a higher position, such as by mounting or putting their muzzle or paw on the underling. You can use a similar signal. Start by putting your dog into a down position for 5 to 10 minutes while you sit comfortably in a chair and read or watch TV. Keep an eye on him and don't let him up or let him crawl away. After he is used to this, slide an arm or leg over him, gently but firmly and without petting him. Also, never let a dominant dog sleep on your bed.

Putting the dog in a down position is also an excellent diagnostic of the dominance relations between you and your dog. If your dog resents being placed down or resents being rolled belly up, you know he is not accepting your leadership without question. That is why you want to introduce these exercises gradually and cautiously, to avoid triggering a fight.

Enroll in an obedience class with your dog. A dog may think he is in control while going for a stroll in a park. If he sniffs and pulls in a certain direction, you may well let him go there, but no such illusion is possible during a heeling pattern. In obedience class, it is clear who is in command and the consequences of a "disagreement"—a jerk on the leash on your part—are also unmistakable.

You are walking about the house and your dog is in the way? Don't give him a wide berth; make him move. Bump into him if he is slow to make room for you. With a more dominant dog, you may even seek out such a situation intentionally. Having to get out of your way to avoid the risk of being stepped on sends your dog the unmistakable message that he is a subordinate and you are the alpha.

If you want to be treated as the leader of the pack by your dog, don't take orders from him. It is up to you to decide when and what to do. For instance, if your dominant dog comes and nudges you, asking to be petted or to play, don't automatically accede to his request. Give him some simple command, and only after he has executed it successfully should you pet him or play with him as a reward. Be sure to stop and gently send him away before he decides he has had enough; you are the alpha and you should decide when the session ends. The same holds for treats— make him work for them. You may require as little as obeying a sit or a down command, but this will make the difference between paying your dog homage versus having him earn a reward by obeying your order.

For the same reason, you should not acquiesce to your dog's dislike of any of your handling, such as brushing, cleaning teeth, clipping nails, giving pills, crating, getting into the car, etc. You should introduce these practices gradually, gently, and with positive reinforcements. But if your dog objects to any of these and you simply back off and accept his, "I don't want to do it" for an answer, you send the wrong signal.

How strictly you ought to follow all of this advice depends on how dominant your dog is. For example, if you are sure your dog completely accepts you as the leader, you might sometimes pet him or slip him a treat without first making him work for it, or you may even elect to let him on your bed, but only at your invitation.

If your dog is dominant and you have practiced these steps regularly but still feel that the dog is challenging you, seek help from experts before the situation escalates any further. You can get referrals from your veterinarian, trainer, or kennel club.

SHYNESS

If your dog behaves shyly, the key to overcoming this behavior is to properly and intensively socialize him. Ideally, you should start from early puppyhood, but even adult shy dogs can improve with socialization. Conversely, a shy dog may backslide when socialization is discontinued.

The basic ideas are the same as with socialization of a puppy. Keep in mind that while gentleness is imperative, it is also essential to avoid either rewarding fearfulness in the mistaken attempt to comfort your scared pet, or giving in and sparing your pet exposure to situations he feels uneasy with. You will have to choose an appropriate combination of encouragement on one hand and firmness and consistency on the other. You will also have to try to push your dog up to, but not beyond, his capabilities of absorbing new experiences and adapting to them. Here, observing your dog and understanding how soft or how resilient he is will make a lot of difference.

Also, keep in mind that dogs go through two fear periods during their first year (generally between 8 and 12 weeks and between 7 and 12 months), and in these periods, they act more fearful and spooky than usual. During these periods, you may want to continue your socialization program, but perhaps reduce its intensity. Do not be discouraged if your dog appears to have backslided from the level of confidence he had previously reached. This is a temporary phenomenon, and the dog should recover with age and continued socialization.

DOG AGGRESSION

Many Canaan Dogs are naturally aggressive toward unfamiliar dogs. This is a breed trait with a strong survival purpose—defending the pack's territory. However, proper socialization can greatly reduce this

This puppy is properly greeting an adult dog. Socialization helps the puppy develop appropriate social skills and reduces the natural tendency of many Canaan Dogs to be aggressive toward unfamiliar dogs.

tendency. Of course, all Canaans can and should be taught to control their behavior and can then be taken without trouble into dog shows or other areas crowded with dogs.

To achieve this, it will often be enough to convey to your Canaan Dog that you disapprove of his growling or trying to attack other dogs. Your dog must first accept you without reservation as his leader and must have had at least some obedience training. You must make sure you are not a contributing factor to his aggressiveness. Perhaps you are tense yourself, and he feels, as a consequence, that the situation must be a threatening one. Without realizing it, you may have tightened his leash, which would restrict his movements and make him feel more vulnerable.

If your dog is more markedly aggressive, he may not pay attention to you but focus on the other dog instead, so conveying your message to him may be more difficult. Be cautious and be prepared. If your dog is very dominant, and you correct him too harshly in order to catch his attention, he may redirect his aggressiveness toward you.

As an alternative to a confrontation with a dominant dog and as a preferred method with a more subordinate dog that may act aggressively out of fear, you may want to divert your dog's attention and focus it elsewhere. For instance, you may give him a heel command and heel him away from the other dog, but not too far—you don't want to run away from the problem, which in the long run would only compound it. Make sure he pays attention to the heeling by performing plenty of curves, changes of pace, etc. Correct him if he is still distracted by the other dog. Because you are correcting him for his sloppy heeling and not for his aggression, he is much less likely to respond negatively. As soon as he starts paying attention to you, praise him lavishly. The lesson is that you clearly disapprove of brawling with other dogs, but that by focusing on you he can get back in your good graces. If you have no room for heeling and/or if your dog is more advanced in obedience, command him to sit and to pay attention to you.

Of course, all this can work only if your dog is on leash or if you have truly excellent voice control of him. If you have a very dog-aggressive Canaan, you might never be able to let him run and play with unfamiliar dogs or with other dogs of the same sex in your own household without supervision.

More independent than average, it is advisable to leave your Canaan Dog in a fenced area when you cannot supervise him, as he may attempt to run away. Velikaya's Mitsav-Ruah, owned by Isabella Zirri, Italy.

RUNNING AWAY

Canaan Dogs are more independent than average. Because of this, they can be left home alone without being overly stressed, and while they are affectionate, they are not cloying. The counterpart, however, is that a few Canaan Dogs have a tendency to run away. Therefore, it is absolutely inadvisable to leave them in an unfenced yard.

Many Canaan Dogs are easily confined by a four-foot high fence. However, a small number of Canaans learn to squeeze or dig underneath fences, open gates, or scale chain-link fences up to six feet high. Some of these problems can be fixed with the appropriate hardware and/or training, but if you have a real escape artist, you may need stronger measures, such as a really secure dog run with a fenced top and a concrete floor. You also can add an electronic fence (with a radio collar) to keep your dog from approaching your regular fence. Using an electronic fence alone is not advisable, especially if there are loose dogs in the neighborhood that might trespass on your dog's territory. Canaan Dogs are so territorial that they may elect to endure the shock in order to chase away the trespassers, and finding themselves on the other side of the fence might escape.

EXCESSIVE BARKING

Actually, Canaan Dogs are very quiet around the house unless sounding the alarm. Not gratuitous barkers, they are always barking at something. Of course, their owners may not always agree that the *something* is worth barking about. This is particularly a problem for city dwellers, where there are more likely to be intruders such as mail carriers, utility workers, and door-to-door salespeople entering the dog's territory. Also, neighbors who might be bothered by the noise are in closer proximity.

You will notice during his adolescence that your once quiet puppy is now barking at everything, including such innocuous objects as a small branch that fell into your yard. As your dog grows older and wiser, he will become more discriminating as to what he warns you about, and the noisiness will diminish somewhat. Out of consideration for your neighbors and your own peace and quiet, you will want to get a handle on this excessive barking early on.

Keep in mind that you want your dog to bark if an intruder enters the house, so what you really hope to accomplish is to train the dog to stop barking excessively. This can be achieved by training your dog to bark on command by telling him to bark in situations where you know he is going to, such as when the mail carrier enters your yard. If you put the behavior on cue, the dog should bark less during times when he has not been commanded to do so. To help diminish barking at other times, establish some ground rules. For example, the dog is allowed four barks while you check the cause for the alarm. Then, when you command him, the dog must cease. Put some coins in a soft drink can, say, "Be quiet!" and rattle the can to startle the dog. As soon as the dog stops barking, praise the dog and distract him with petting, a toy, or a treat so that he will not resume barking.

During this training process, there is much you can do to spare the neighbors. Keep your dog indoors when you are not at home. When you *are* home, bring the dog indoors if he starts to bark excessively. Visual barriers, such as window curtains or blinds and privacy fences, will keep your Canaan Dog from detecting everything that passes. A radio or stereo may mask some outside noises.

You will observe that what really sets off a Canaan Dog is something that isn't where it is supposed to be. They will react to stray cats, stray dogs, a new dog next door, or new neighbors. After a few days, when your dog learns that the new dog next door or the new neighbors are there to stay, he will stop sounding the alarm whenever he sees them; they now belong.

THE VERSATILE CANAAN DOG

Canaan Dogs are an incredibly versatile breed. Although they have never been selectively bred for service to humans, Canaan Dogs are valued for the traits that they come by naturally, and these have been put to a number of uses in the service of humankind. Dr. Menzel was asked to provide dogs for military work, and Canaan Dogs were quite suited for a variety of these tasks because of their keen senses, intelligence, and hardiness. The breed was used for mine detection and message delivery and are still used by the Israeli army for patrol and sentry work. They guard military installations, kibbutzim, factories, etc. Bedouin and Arab villagers continue to use Canaans to guard their camps, flocks, and other possessions.

Today, Canaan Dogs participate in a number of events and service-related activities. Although the breed has only been recognized relatively recently, they have already earned advanced performance titles.

Canaan Dogs are an incredibly versatile breed. Because of their keen senses, intelligence, and hardiness, they are naturally suited to a variety of tasks. Mello, owned by Isabella Zirri, Italy.

VERSATILITY

HERDING

Legend has it that Canaan Dogs descended from the herding and flock guardian dogs of the ancient Hebrews. We'll probably never know if the ancient Hebrews actually used the ancestors of Canaan Dogs for herding— in spite of all the references to flocks and shepherds in the Bible, wild dogs, but not herding dogs, are mentioned. Until Dr. Menzel created the modern breed, Arabs and the Bedouins were the primary owners of semi-domesticated Canaan Dogs, and in these cultures, women and children did the herding, so there has been no selection for herding ability over the past 2000 years or so. About half of all Canaan Dogs tested in the US do show some herding instinct. But many are one-day wonders that show interest in sheep on first contact and then never again, in spite of repeated opportunities. Only about half of those displaying instinct have the drive and focus needed to mold a functional helper for the farm. When prospective buyers tell us they must have a Canaan Dog that will herd, we warn them to look for an older dog with demonstrated instinct, or else they are apt to be disappointed. Some Canaan Dogs have earned herding titles from various organizations.

GUARDING

Without a doubt, Canaan Dogs are superb flock guardians. Their keen senses coupled with the territoriality and pack loyalty common to wild dogs makes them naturally suited to this job. They will defend the pack, the pack's territory, and its possessions. In Israel, both the military and civilians use them for guarding purposes.

Canaan Dogs guard by sounding the alarm whenever anything unusual or potentially dangerous is seen, and they can spot such objects at great distances. Canaan Dogs typically circle intruders and bark ferociously. They have a strong sense of self-preservation, however, and usually keep a safe distance rather than launching an attack unless absolutely necessary. Canaan Dogs don't attack humans except under extreme provocation. Their vigorous barking is usually impressive enough to accomplish the objective without force.

Only one Canaan Dog that we know of has been trained for protection work, but most put on a pretty good show, even without formal training. One Canaan Dog stood down a man who was brandishing a knife. She placed herself between her owner and the attacker and barked threateningly whenever he tried to advance. Another owner's house was the only one on the block

Legend has it that Canaan Dogs are descended from the flock-guarding and herding dogs of the ancient Hebrews. Cherrysh Levi ben Trapper, owned by Sheryl Glass, demonstrates his herding ability.

not broken into because their Canaan Dog gave alarm.

THERAPY AND SERVICE DOG WORK

Dr. Menzel trained several Canaan Dogs as seeing eye dogs, but most are not well-suited for the task because of their reactivity to strange sights, sounds, and unfamiliar dogs. Yet several of our more outgoing Canaans are proving to be excellent therapy dogs. The same dog that protected her owner from the knife-wielding man, Keely, has been a certified Delta Society® PetPartner® for three years. She makes weekly visits to a hospice where she accompanies the ambulatory clients on walks, volunteers to be brushed, entertains with her tricks, and makes herself available for petting. Several other Canaan Dogs have been certified by Therapy Dogs International and make hospital rounds. Having your dog evaluated by one of these national organizations is advisable. Not all Canaan Dogs are suited for such activity, nor would they enjoy it. These national organizations provide training for the human member of the team and liability insurance.

OBEDIENCE

Several organizations award obedience titles. There are various levels of competition, with the most basic demonstrating skills such as heeling, coming on command, and staying, and the advanced levels additionally requiring jumping, retrieving, and scent work. Attend an obedience trial to get a feel for the sport. Even if you have no intention of competing formally, some level of obedience training is advisable. Obedience training ensures quality time is spent with your dog, establishes your authority with your dog, creates a well-behaved companion, and deepens the relationship between you. Your local kennel club might offer obedience classes, and there are many private trainers and many books on the subject. Kennel club classes are often a good way to begin, with private trainers providing the polish for formal competition. Ask around for recommendations. Canaan Dogs can do quite well in obedience competition. A number have basic titles, and several have earned advanced titles and competed successfully in tournaments as well.

TRACKING

Wild Canaan Dogs have to use their tracking skills to find food, water, and mates. With the keen senses they have inherited, domestic Canaan Dogs can do well in tracking tests. In this sport, dogs follow a scent laid by someone who walks a track in order to find articles dropped by that person. Wild Canaan Dogs have to remain aware of their entire surroundings, and therefore their domesticated descendants can sometimes become distracted while on the track. This has not prevented several Canaan Dogs from earning basic tracking titles.

AGILITY

One of the fastest growing dog sports is agility, a sport in which dogs navigate an obstacle course under their owner's direction. There are quite a few organizations

Attentive and loyal companions, some Canaans prove to be excellent therapy dogs. Keely is a certified PetPartner® and makes weekly visits to a hospice.

Natural athletes, Canaans can excel in any style of agility. U-AGII Keely's Girl Tobie, NA CGC, owned by Lee Boyd, performs the tire jump with ease.

that offer titles. Some styles of agility emphasize control in negotiating the obstacles, while others emphasize speed over precision. Canaan Dogs are natural athletes and can do quite well in any style of agility, although an individual dog may be more suited to one style than another. Several Canaan Dogs have earned agility titles, and most of these have titles from more than one organization and have progressed to advanced levels of competition. Agility is quite equipment-intensive, so you will probably need to find a club where you can take classes using their equipment. Look for a trial in your area to become familiar with the sport and research the local clubs where you might train.

THE BREED RING

Breeders show their breeding stock in the conformation ring at a dog show. Here, dogs of the same breed compete against one another, and a judge picks a winner from each class based on how well the dog compares to the ideal structure, movement, and temperament described in that breed's standard. The winners of each class then compete to determine the best of breed at the show that day. Winners earn points toward their championship title. The best specimen of that breed then goes on to compete against the best dogs of other breeds in what is called the group ring. Once the best of each group is chosen, these dogs compete against one another for the best dog in the entire show.

To be eligible to compete, your dog must be registered with the national or international organization offering the show, should be of show quality (a good specimen of the breed), and must be intact (not spayed

73

or neutered, as these dogs represent breeding stock).

If you have a show-quality dog, especially if you intend to breed, you should take some handling classes and enter your dog in breed competition. Handling classes teach you how to present your dog to a judge and are usually offered by a local kennel club.

Canaan Dogs have earned championship titles from all of the principal registries, such as the American Kennel Club (AKC) and the United Kennel Club (UKC) and placed best in their group, as well as an occasional Best in Show.

HIKING, CAMPING, AND CANOEING

By all means, include your dog in your vacation whenever possible. Canaan Dogs make superb hiking and camping companions. Include your dog in your conditioning program when readying for extensive hikes. Most national parks do not allow dogs on trails, but national and state forests usually permit leashed dogs. Call before you go to verify that dogs are welcome. Please practice responsible dog ownership, so that the privilege of being able to have our pets accompany us is not rescinded. Keep your dog on leash so that he does not harass wildlife, livestock, and other campers. Pick up your dog's droppings. Remember to carry enough water for both you and your pet.

Most Canaan Dogs enjoy swimming and wading, and several owners have trained their dogs to ride in canoes.

Other Activities

One Canaan Dog has been trained to pull a cart—certainly not a traditional use of the breed, but one which he seems to enjoy! Most adult Canaan Dogs are not toy fanatics, and we don't yet know of any Canaan Dog flyball competitors, but some do enjoy playing Frisbee. Their historical uses, keen senses, athleticism, intelligence, and ability to think for themselves make Canaan Dogs suited for search and rescue work, but none that we know of have recently been trained in that capacity.

FINAL THOUGHTS

Some final thoughts about Canaan Dogs and competitive sports: Canaan Dogs are incredibly clever and agile and can be trained to do just about anything. If you are looking for a versatile breed that excels in a variety of sports, this may be the breed for you. On the other hand, if you are looking for a dog that will be a top-notch competitor and withstand extensive campaigning, this may not be your breed. A Canaan Dog's reliability can be a little iffy because of their independent nature; they always want to know, "What's in it for me?" Because they are intelligent, senseless repetition bores them. Their keen senses and reactive nature mean that many experience sensory overload, leading to mental fatigue in the unfamiliar, noisy, and crowded conditions common at shows. This is not to say that you can't do well with a Canaan Dog in competition; obviously many have. These owners discovered where their dog's talents lie and learned how to bring out the best in their dog. Accept your dog as the unique individual that he is and train him because of the benefits of mental and physical exercise, because it will make your dog a better companion. Train because you both enjoy it and because of the deep bond that will develop between the two of you as a result. By all means, participate in formal competition if you desire. Just keep a proper perspective. The sport is never more important than the dog.

To avoid boring your brilliant Canaan Dog—cross-train! Dabble in a variety of sports, even if one is your mainstay. As an example of one of the many benefits, you'll find that basic obedience gives you the control needed to guide your dog through an agility course and agility training makes off-lead obedience heeling seem much less scary. Above all, have fun yourself and make sure your dog is enjoying it as well!

Canaan Dogs have earned conformation championship titles from all the principal registries worldwide. Ch. Bay Path's Amitz CGC, owned by Cheryl and Jerry Hennings and Sandra Fournier, won Best of Breed at the 1998 and 1999 ICDCA National Specialty.

HEALTH CONCERNS OF THE CANAAN DOG

In addition to all of the other attractive things about Canaan Dogs, they are one of the healthiest breeds in existence. For example, bloat and bleeding disorders are unheard of in Canaan Dogs. We have natural selection to thank for this, as only the healthiest, most fit pariah dogs lived long enough to reproduce. It is up to every Canaan Dog owner and breeder to preserve this legacy so that the Canaan Dog does not become rife with genetic problems, as has happened to so many other breeds.

The following disorders have been clinically diagnosed in Canaan Dogs. None of these disorders is common; all afflict less than 5 percent of the world population of Canaan Dogs. Dogs with any of these disorders should not be used for breeding, as these afflictions usually have an inherited basis.

HIP DYSPLASIA

Hip dysplasia is a condition in which the ball-and-socket joint of the hip is not properly formed. One or both hips can be affected. The degree of dysplasia varies from mild to severe. In mild cases, the dog may never have an outward manifestation of the problem; indeed, one Canaan Dog with a mildly dysplastic hip went on to earn several agility titles with no sign of unsoundness. In severe cases, the dog may become crippled as he ages and extensive surgery may be required. Several organizations use radiographs to evaluate a dog's hips. The Orthopedic Foundation for Animals (OFA) and PennHIP use different techniques and ages of evaluation. The OFA is the older organization and therefore has the more extensive database on Canaan Dogs. Thanks to natural selection, the breed has one of the lowest incidences of hip dysplasia. Most dogs receive a Good or Excellent rating from OFA; fewer receive a rating of Fair, and less than 4 percent of dogs whose radiographs are submitted are evaluated as dysplastic.

EPILEPSY

Of all the disorders listed here, epilepsy is the most difficult for owners to cope with, as it afflicts the dog throughout much of his life. Seizures may or may not be able to be controlled with medication. There are different forms of epilepsy. In the Canaan Dog, there is clearly an inherited form of epilepsy, but seizures can be due to environmental causes as well, such as head trauma. Prospective buyers of Canaan Dogs should request health charts listing afflicted animals from the health chair of the breed club and avoid dogs closely related to afflicted individuals.

EYE PROBLEMS

Earlier in the history of the breed, progressive retinal atrophy (PRA) was discovered in a few bloodlines. PRA causes the dog to gradually become blind. This disorder seems to have been largely eradicated in Canaan Dogs at present, but it is prudent to continue to have dogs evaluated. Without evaluation, the disease may not be detected until later in life, after the dog has reproduced and passed the defect to the offspring. Thus, it is particularly important that all breeding stock be evaluated, which involves ophthalmic examination by a specialist. Such specialists are on staff at veterinary colleges and may hold screening clinics in conjunction with dog shows.

A few Canaan Dogs have developed cataracts before reaching old age.

AUTOIMMUNE DISORDERS

Canaan Dogs seem somewhat prone to autoimmune disorders. An autoimmune disorder results when the body fails to recognize its own tissues and mounts an immune response against those tissues. It is probable that some dogs have a genetic predisposition upon which an environmental factor acts to tip the scale, so that an autoimmune reaction results. Wild and semi-domesticated Canaan Dogs receive no veterinary care, so a vigilant immune system is beneficial to their survival. This hair-trigger immune system may get domesticated Canaan Dogs into trouble. One should not overvaccinate Canaan Dogs, as vaccines contain antigens meant to stimulate the immune system. Certainly all dogs should be vaccinated, but many vaccines should not be given simultaneously or at too short an interval.

The most common autoimmune disorders of Canaan Dogs are hypothyroidism, Addison's disease, and male sterility. In the most common form of hypothyroidism, the thyroid gland has been attacked and is underfunctioning. The dog will have a low metabolic rate and therefore little energy. It will be less tolerant of cool temperatures and might have a poor, dull coat. Hypothyroidism is relatively easy to treat through daily oral medication.

Addison's disease results from damage to the adrenal glands. The dog is intolerant of stress and may vomit, drink excessively, and have a poor appetite. If untreated, this disease can be fatal. The disease can often be controlled through medication and minimizing stress, but treatment is somewhat expensive and not universally effective.

The immune system of male dogs may also attack the male's sperm-producing cells, leaving him infertile. Fortunately, there are no other side effects, so no treatment is necessary.

CRYPTORCHIDISM

Cryptorchidism refers to undescended testicles of the male. Either one or both testes may fail to descend into the scrotum. The retained testes must be surgically removed, because of a high probability that they will develop tumors. Even if one testis has descended, the male should be neutered, as the genetic predisposition for this disorder means that this particular dog should not be bred.

It is up to *all* of us to keep the Canaan Dog breed healthy. You can do your part by buying puppies from parents who have been screened for genetic disorders. Even if you do not intend to breed, consider having your dog evaluated after it matures. This adds to the database for the breed and lets breeders know if they have any as yet undetected problems in their bloodlines. Report any health problems to your dog's breeder and to the national breed club's health chair. If the problem has a genetic basis and you have not already done so, please spay or neuter your dog. Breeding would just perpetuate the problem and is hard on a dog with health problems anyway. Only the best, healthiest dogs should be bred if we want to preserve the legacy left to the breed by many centuries of natural selection.

YOUR HEALTHY CANAAN DOG

Canaan Dogs, like all other animals, are capable of contracting illnesses that in many cases are readily avoided by sound husbandry. Well-bred and well-cared-for animals are less prone to developing diseases. Remember that an ounce of prevention is worth a pound of cure. Your veterinarian is the best person to assist you in this. If you haven't already selected a veterinarian, ask

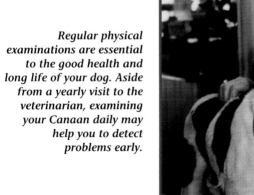

Regular physical examinations are essential to the good health and long life of your dog. Aside from a yearly visit to the veterinarian, examining your Canaan daily may help you to detect problems early.

friends for recommendations. A veterinarian in whom you have confidence is a comforting asset.

PHYSICAL EXAMS

Your dog should receive a regular physical examination by a veterinarian at least once a year, generally when he receives his annual vaccinations. But in addition to that, you should examine your dog daily, starting at the head and working your way around the body. Look for any sign of lesions or external parasites such as fleas or ticks. Remove any burrs or thorns lodged in the coat or paws. Apart from the fact that your examination will detect problems at an early stage, it is an excellent way of socializing a puppy to being handled.

HEALTHY TEETH AND GUMS

Chewing is instinctive. Puppies chew so that their teeth and jaws grow strong and healthy. It is important for puppies to develop bite inhibition, a process by which puppies learn to control the pressure with which they bite. This is why puppies have such needle-sharp teeth. If they bite a playmate too hard, it hurts! The playmate refuses to play anymore and the pup learns to be more careful and use less pressure if he wants to continue playing.

As the puppy's deciduous (baby) teeth fall out and the permanent teeth begin to erupt, the puppy will need something safe to chew to aid the teething process. However, even after the adult teeth are fully emerged, the chewing instinct does not fade. Adult dogs instinctively chew to clean their teeth, massage their gums, and exercise their jaws.

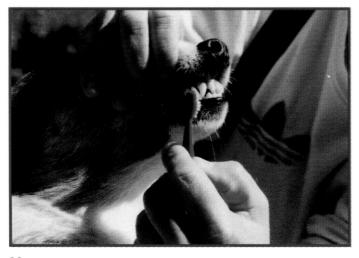

Healthy teeth and gums are important to the well-being of your Canaan Dog. Check and brush his teeth regularly.

As with humans, it is essential for your dog to have clean teeth. Your veterinarian will examine your dog's mouth during the annual exam and tell you if your dog needs to have his teeth cleaned. Although dogs do not get cavities in the same way humans do, their teeth accumulate plaque and tartar. The accumulation of plaque and tartar must be removed, or it will irritate the gums and erode the surface of the teeth. The dog will have bad breath, and if left untreated, gingivitis and periodontitis will cause the loss of teeth. Another danger is that the oral bacteria at these sites of infection will migrate to internal organs causing damage there.

If the veterinarian has to scale your dog's teeth, or worse, remove diseased teeth, the dog will have to be sedated. Again, prevention is the cheaper and safer alternative. You can brush your dog's teeth just as you do your own. Use toothpaste formulated especially for pets, available in most pet stores and mail-order pet supply catalogs. You can use one of your old toothbrushes or buy one designed for pets. Most dogs don't find the taste of the toothpaste objectionable, even licking it off the brush, but need to get used to having a brush in their mouth. If you make this a pleasurable experience, the dogs will come to accept this as routine. One owner we know has a Canaan Dog that tolerates an electric toothbrush in his mouth! By the way, brushing your dog's teeth is a good way to help him maintain a soft mouth (bite inhibition), as he gets used to having your fingers in and around his mouth. You should make it a practice to brush daily, but several times a week is sufficient to keep tartar at bay.

An additional strategy to maintain oral hygiene is to provide your dog with something safe to chew. Chew toys not only keep the dog's teeth clean but also relieve stress and provide the dog with entertainment.

There are many products to choose from, and obviously you want to provide something safe. If you have a local butcher, you can ask for bones. You want a strong bone, such as a thigh bone that won't splinter when chewed, as splinters can perforate a dog's digestive tract or cause blockage. For this reason, do not cook the bones before giving them to your dog, because cooked bones splinter more easily. Or you can now buy sterilized or smoked bones in pet stores. After your dog's interest in these bones wanes, you can revive it by filling the marrow cavity of the bone

Chew toys not only keep your Canaan's teeth clean, but also relieve stress and provide your dog with entertainment.

with delectable treats such as peanut butter, suet, dog food kibble, cheese, bread, or biscuit pieces.

Many other chew products abound, such as hooves, pigs' ears, and rawhide chews in various shapes and sizes. Our dogs enjoy all of these and we have not personally had a problem with any of them. However, we know of a Canaan Dog that swallowed a large piece of rawhide and the resultant bowel obstruction required surgery. Keep in mind that there may be a slight risk with some chews, but it may be greatly outweighed by the benefits of oral hygiene and entertainment. Ask your veterinarian what products they recommend. During the course of their practice, they will have developed an awareness of any product causing recurrent problems.

FIGHTING FLEAS

Fleas are insects that are external parasites of pets. They may be red, brown, or black in color and hop from place to place. The adults suck the blood of the host; in this case, your dog. Eggs may be laid on the puppy or more commonly in carpet and bedding. The eggs hatch in 4 to 21 days, depending on the temperature, but they can survive for up to 18 months if conditions are not currently favorable. The eggs hatch into larvae that are maggot-like and molt several times as they mature. The larvae feed on fecal material from the adult fleas, which is rich in blood. This fecal material is often called "flea dirt." It is a prime indicator of the presence of fleas and can be seen as blackish specks the size of ground pepper in the dog's coat. When brushed out and placed in water, these flecks dissolve and the blood content becomes more apparent. The larvae form pupae that can survive long periods until suitable temperature or the presence of a host causes them to emerge as adult fleas and continue the life cycle.

Flea bites itch and cause the dog to scratch. Some dogs are allergic to fleas and develop flea bite dermatitis, which persists after the fleas are eradicated. In addition, fleas can transmit infections and parasites to your pet. It is important to control fleas as soon as they appear on your dog.

A variety of flea baths and sprays are available for pet, home, and yard, but many have hazardous side effects to living organisms if misused, making them potentially dangerous pollutants of your home and neighborhood. If a flea infestation is discovered early, it can often be controlled by washing the animals' bedding and vacuuming several times a week. Houses with hardwood floors provide fewer hiding places for fleas than those with extensive carpeting. You can buy metal flea combs with closely set teeth. These will make it through most Canaan Dogs' coats, permitting you to comb out fleas. Recently, topical medications have been developed that when applied to a small spot on the dog's back, and absorbed by the dog's body, are very efficacious against fleas. Some have the added bonus of also killing ticks. Because they are applied to such a small area and have longer effectiveness, there are fewer environmental hazards from these products. There are also products administered orally that keep fleas at bay. Ask your veterinarian which product they recommend and follow directions carefully.

There are many parasites, like fleas and ticks, that your dog may encounter when playing outside. Be sure to check your Canaan's coat thoroughly when he comes in from the outdoors. Venla, owned by Isabella Zirri, Italy.

TICKS

Ticks are arthropods that have eight legs, as do their distant relatives, the spiders. Ticks bury their mouthparts into the skin of their host and gorge on its blood. Some ticks are species-specific for a certain host, while others are more adaptable and parasitize many species. The size of a tick depends on its species, age, and the length of time spent feeding. Some small species are the size of a pinhead, while others, when fully engorged, swell to approach a small coin in size.

Not only can ticks make dogs anemic by robbing them of blood, but they also can transmit a variety of diseases such as Lyme disease. Lyme disease can cripple a dog or person. The disease is named for Lyme, Connecticut, where it was first detected, but has now been diagnosed in most regions of the US.

Dogs pick up ticks while hiking in forests and tall grass, but of course, ticks can also be carried to your yard by other pets or wildlife in the neighborhood. During tick season, you should examine your dog frequently. After a hike, immediately combing your dog with a flea comb may remove ticks before they have a chance to attach. If you find an attached tick, the best way to remove it is to dab the tick with a strong salt solution, iodine, or alcohol. This will cause them to loosen their hold, at which time they can be removed with tweezers or your fingers. Daub the site where they were attached with antibiotic ointment.

If ticks are common in your area, consult with your vet about the topical applications that are absorbed into the dog's body to kill external parasites. Make sure you use one that kills both fleas and ticks, rather than just fleas.

SKIN DISORDERS

Apart from problems associated with lesions created by biting pests, a puppy may fall victim to a number of other skin disorders. Examples are ringworm, mange, and eczema. Ringworm is not caused by a worm at all, but rather a fungus. It manifests itself as one or more bald circles. Ringworm is easily diagnosed by your veterinarian and easily treated with modern medications.

Mange is a general term applied to skin conditions caused by mites. The mites either live in hair follicles that they destroy or burrow just beneath the skin and feed on the living tissue or skin debris. The dog's fur

The importance of consulting a veterinarian on the diagnosis of internal disorders cannot be overemphasized—for example, a relatively common problem, such as diarrhea, could also be a sign of something more serious. CHF Israeli Jewel, owned by Sherly Glass.

falls out, and a flaky crust develops on the skin. The skin itches, so the dog scratches himself, which is worse than the original condition, because it opens lesions that are then vulnerable to bacterial or fungal infection. It is essential to identify the type of mange mite involved before an effective treatment can be determined, and this is a job for your veterinarian.

Eczema is a nonspecific term applied to many skin disorders. Sunburn, toxic chemical exposure, allergies, hormone imbalance, and even stress can contribute to deterioration of the skin and coat. Given so many possible causes, it is important to enlist your veterinarian's help in determining the source of the problem. It may be a case of taking each possibility at a time and trying to eliminate it as a contributing factor, so as to pinpoint the source of the problem.

INTERNAL DISORDERS

We can't overemphasize the importance of consulting a veterinarian on the diagnosis of internal disorders. A relatively common and simple problem such as diarrhea might be caused by nothing more serious than overeating or switching to a different food. Conversely, it might represent something far more serious. In any case, persistent diarrhea causes dehydration and acid-base imbalance, which is potentially life threatening. It is up to your veterinarian to make the correct diagnosis.

The following symptoms, especially if persistent, occurring in combination, or added to in progression, mean that you should visit the veterinarian right away.

Continual Vomiting

All dogs vomit from time to time and may eat grass to induce vomiting. This is a self-medicating behavior common to many carnivores. However, continued vomiting is a clear sign of a problem. It may be due to a blockage in your puppy's gastrointestinal tract, or it could be caused by worms or any number of other problems.

Diarrhea

This, too, may be transient and not much cause for concern. When you first bring your puppy home, the travel and stress of adjustment to new home and food can trigger diarrhea. But if diarrhea persists for more than 48 hours or if there is blood in the feces, take the dog to the vet immediately. Puppies, in particular, can dehydrate very quickly.

Runny Eyes or Nose

These may be signs of allergy or respiratory infection. If the discharge does not clear up in a few days, especially if it looks thick and milky rather than clear, take your puppy to the veterinarian.

Coughing and Wheezing

Prolonged coughing can be a sign of respiratory or heart problems. If the pup makes a wheezing sound, he is having difficulty breathing and should be examined for respiratory problems.

Cries When Attempting to Urinate or Defecate

This might represent minor constipation or more serious problems such as bowel obstructions or bladder infections.

Cries When Touched

If you are handling the puppy gently and he cries anytime pressure is applied to a given area of the body, this indicates a problem that must be diagnosed by your vet.

Refuses Food

Generally, puppies and dogs are greedy eaters. A few are more fussy, but none should refuse food for more than a day. If they remain uninterested for longer, something is not as it should be, and it is worth consulting your vet.

General Listlessness

All dogs have off days when they do not seem their usual selves. If this condition persists for more than a couple of days, the dog should be examined by a professional. There are many diseases that can develop with few outward signs. Blood, fecal, or other

All dogs have off days when they do not seem themselves. However, if this lethargic condition persists for several days, you should have your Canaan examined by a professional.

tests may be needed to identify the disorder. Many observant owners save their dog's life by getting him to a veterinarian for help before a life-threatening disease reaches an advanced state that may not be treatable.

Worms

There are many species of worms, and a number of these live in dogs. Many create no problem at all, so you are not even aware that they are present. Others can be tolerated in small quantities, but become a major problem if there are more than a few. The most common types seen in dogs are tapeworms and roundworms.

Tapeworms are diagnosed by observing tiny objects that look like grains of dried rice sticking to the fur around the puppy's anus. They may also be observed on feces, and if freshly deposited, may be moving weakly. These are sacs that contain the eggs of the tapeworm. The eggs are eaten by rabbits, rodents, or fleas, which serve as intermediate hosts. The eggs develop into a larval stage in this host, and the host must then be eaten by the dog in order to infect him and complete the life cycle. Unless you allow your dog to roam and hunt, which is inadvisable, the most common source of infection will be fleas. The flea bites your dog, the dog bites at the itch and ingests the flea, and the larvae it contains will develop into adult tapeworms in the dog's intestines. Most tapeworms are relatively benign parasites, unless the infestation is extremely heavy. Adult tapeworms lack their own digestive tract; instead they rob the puppy of food he has begun digesting. Your veterinarian can provide you with very effective wormers to free the puppy of these parasites.

Roundworms of the species *Toxocara canis* can infest dogs. They are thin and may grow to a length of 8 inches (20 cm), and therefore look like a piece of spaghetti. The worms feed on digesting food in the pup's intestines. In chronic cases, the puppy will become pot-bellied, have diarrhea, and may vomit. At first, the pup will always be hungry, but eventually may stop eating if the worms have become numerous enough to debilitate the puppy or block his digestive tract. The worms lay eggs in the puppy and these pass out in the feces. The eggs remain infective in the soil for a long time and can be eaten by this puppy or another to complete the life cycle. Larval worms can also migrate within pregnant bitches and be passed across the placenta to her puppies before birth. Bitches should be checked for worms before breeding, and pups wormed a few weeks after birth.

Hookworms are another type of roundworm that can make puppies anemic by sucking blood from lesions that they create in the wall of the digestive tract. Whipworms are another common intestinal roundworm of puppies. Heavy infestations may cause weight loss, diarrhea, and anemia.

These roundworms are diagnosed by taking a stool sample from your puppy to your veterinarian for examination. The presence of worms and their identity is determined by looking for their eggs in the feces. The dog is then wormed accordingly. Worming is a simple process but may need to be repeated in order to eliminate all life stages of the worm. As roundworms are often transmitted through fecal contamination, cleaning up feces promptly from your yard and washing your hands thoroughly after handling soil so that you do not spread the contamination will help break the life cycle.

There is a very different and deadly type of roundworm that must be mentioned. Heartworms are transmitted by mosquitoes. As their name implies, adult heartworms can lodge in the dog's heart and lead to weight loss and heart, liver, and kidney failure. Unless you live in one of the few places in this country where there are no mosquitoes, you will want to protect your dog from heartworms. When you take your puppy to your veterinarian for the first time, ask about starting the puppy on heartworm preventative. This is a simple, daily or monthly oral medication that dogs readily consume. A heartworm preventative program should not be initiated for adult dogs until a veterinary exam has been performed, because complications from the preventative can result if the dog has already been infected by heartworms. Veterinarians detect the presence of heartworms in unprotected dogs by drawing a small blood sample and using a microscope to look for larval stages in the blood. If infected, prompt treatment is essential to save the dog's life, but at great expense and some risk.

VACCINATIONS

All dogs should be vaccinated against the major canine diseases. Depending on the age of the puppy, your breeder will probably have started the first series of vaccinations and should provide information on what shots the puppy had and when.

Newborn puppies are protected by antibodies received from the mother via her milk. By 8 to 12 weeks of age, that immunity is wearing off and the puppy needs to develop his own immunity. Vaccines are either killed microbes or live milder forms that are given in small doses to stimulate the immune system so that it will be prepared to deal with more serious naturally occurring attacks by these agents in the future. If the immune system does not encounter these diseases naturally, the ability of the immune system to recognize these microbes will diminish over time. That is why booster vaccinations are needed periodically throughout the dog's life to keep the immune system on the alert.

When you receive your puppy, you should contact your veterinarian to find out what the vaccination schedule should be for pups of that age and make an

At 8 to 12 weeks of age, the immunity your puppy received from his mother is wearing off and he'll need to develop his own protection against contagious canine diseases.

appointment to come in for the next series of shots. Puppies' immune systems are maturing and they will need a series of shots repeated over the course of several months. As adults, they will need a booster only once a year.

By the time he is four months old, your puppy should be vaccinated against the deadly rabies virus, which also can infect humans. In many places it is illegal for your dog not to be vaccinated against rabies. This is to protect your dog, your family, and the rest of the animal population from this deadly virus that infects the nervous system and causes dementia and death.

Remember that because of his wild heritage, the Canaan Dog has a very active immune system, and that autoimmune diseases have been known to occur in some individuals. Discuss with your vet the need not to overvaccinate Canaan Dogs. Puppies commonly receive vaccination against distemper, hepatitis, leptospirosis, parainfluenza, and parvovirus administered together in a "cocktail." For Canaan Dogs, it might be better to separate these vaccines and not give them all on the same day. Also, these shots are typically given at 6 weeks, when the efficacy is questionable, and repeated every 3 to 4 weeks until 16 weeks of age to make sure they take effect. Explore the idea of skipping one of the earlier rounds of the series with your veterinarian.

Recently, veterinary colleges have begun recommending against vaccinating puppies for leptospirosis. This disease is uncommon, and the leptospirosis vaccine produces more adverse reactions than most other vaccines. Coronavirus and Lyme disease vaccinations are also not recommended. If your dog is to be in contact with a large number of other dogs at dog shows, training classes, boarding kennels, etc., it might be worthwhile to have him vaccinated against kennel cough, a respiratory infection that is highly contagious, although seldom fatal.

ACCIDENTS

All puppies receive their share of bumps and bruises due to the rather energetic way they play. These will usually heal themselves over a few days. Small cuts should be bathed with a disinfectant and then smeared with antiseptic ointment. If a cut looks more serious, staunch the flow of blood with a towel (duct tape can hold it over the wound in the car) and rush the pup to the veterinarian.

In case of burns, you should apply cold water or an ice pack to the surface. If the burn was due to a chemical, then this must be washed away with copious amounts of cold water. Trim away the fur around the burn if needed and apply antibiotic ointment. If the burn is of a large size, wrap the dog in a blanket and rush him to the vet. Depending on the severity of the burn, the dog may go into shock, which is very dangerous, and the reason the dog must receive immediate veterinary attention.

Do not let your pup jump up and down from heights, as this can cause considerable shock to the joints. Like all youngsters, puppies do not know when enough is enough, so you must be prepared to supervise.

If a broken limb is suspected, try to keep the animal as still as possible. Wrap him in a blanket to restrict movement and get him to a veterinarian immediately.

If you provide a hygienic, puppy-proofed environment and you make daily checks on your puppy's physical state, you have done as much as you can to safeguard him during the most vulnerable period. Routine visits to your veterinarian are also recommended, as the vet may notice something that did not seem important to you. There are dog first aid books available and it might be wise to purchase one to keep at home.

YOUR OLDER DOG

Canaan Dogs are a long-lived breed, and many reach the ripe old age of 14. A few have even made it to 16 or 17 years of age.

If your Canaan Dog becomes ill or sustains an injury from an accident or fall, acting quickly and appropriately can save his life. Kibbe, owned by Phil Saigh, Jr.

The aging process is so gradual that you may not notice it has begun. Your companion will sleep a bit more, tire more easily, and begin to go gray around the muzzle. Some hearing loss may be noticeable. Over the years, you will have developed a special bond with your dog. Now is the time to treasure your remaining years with your friend and help him deal with the aging process.

Of course, regular veterinary checkups will continue to be important. Canaan Dogs are considered to be senior citizens at age eight to ten. A geriatric screening at this age might be a good idea. Your veterinarian will have a blood sample evaluated, and the baseline values obtained while the dog is healthy can provide a comparison to help diagnose problems as the dog continues to age.

A good-quality diet is important throughout your dog's life, and as your dog approaches the age of eight, you should consider switching him to a dog food specifically formulated for geriatric dogs. These are often referred to as senior diets. They contain high-quality protein that is easily digested and lesser amounts of salt to spare the kidneys. The fat content is lower to prevent obesity as the dog becomes less active. Obesity is a serious problem, because it can aggravate heart and joint disease. Increased fiber content helps to maintain proper bowel motility and gives the dog a sense of being replete without consuming so many calories.

Older Canaan Dogs still need regular moderate exercise to stay in shape and prevent boredom. Use your good judgment in evaluating what level to maintain. Older more sedate dogs may make good therapy animals and bring joy to others while visiting hospitals and nursing homes. Taking on a useful job around the house, like fetching the paper, can keep them mentally and physically active.

Older dogs tend to be creatures of habit, and as their sensory capabilities decline, daily routine and a stable environment become more important to them. Feed your dog at the same time and place daily, and take him for walks on a regular schedule. If incontinence develops, see your veterinarian to discuss the source of the problem; there are medications that can help.

With your veterinarian's help, you will know when your dog's quality of life is not what it should be. Euthanasia is a merciful alternative to prolonged suffering; it is quick and seemingly painless, with the animal appearing to fall into a deep sleep until breathing ceases. Your veterinarian can advise you on whether it is possible in your community to bring your dog home to be buried. In some towns, there is a portion of the human cemetery reserved for pets or special cemeteries entirely for pets. Your veterinarian would also be able to dispose of your pet's body should you wish them to make the arrangements.

After a period of mourning, you may wish to consider obtaining another dog. Keep in mind that dogs are individuals, and you will never find another dog that will exactly replace your old one. Your new dog should be appreciated in his own right for his own qualities. It is often said that the best tribute to an old dog is to give another dog a good home.

Your older dog has been a valued family member for a long time, so you'll want to ensure that he enjoys good health and a quality lifestyle. Nine-year-old Tiki, owned by Jerry Hennings, is alert and ready for a romp.

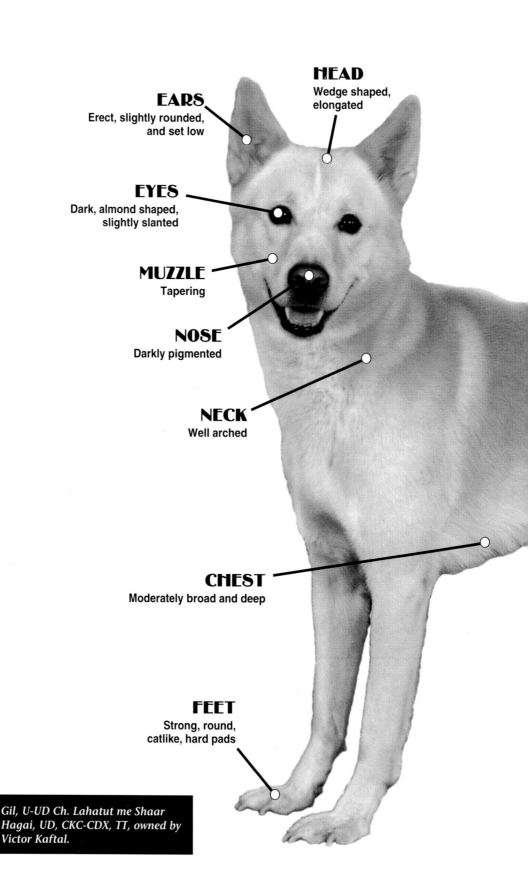

HEAD
Wedge shaped,
elongated

EARS
Erect, slightly rounded,
and set low

EYES
Dark, almond shaped,
slightly slanted

MUZZLE
Tapering

NOSE
Darkly pigmented

NECK
Well arched

CHEST
Moderately broad and deep

FEET
Strong, round,
catlike, hard pads

Gil, U-UD Ch. Lahatut me Shaar Hagai, UD, CKC-CDX, TT, owned by Victor Kaftal.